INSIDE TROPICAL HOMES

DREAMS COME TRUE

INSIDE TROPICAL HOMES

DREAMS COME TRUE

SIBYLLE KRAMER

BRAUN

In the broad expanses of the tropics, architectural masterpieces express a unique symbiosis between humans and nature. This volume dives into the world of tropical residential architecture, where the boundaries between interior and exterior are blurred and human creativity is in harmony with the green heartbeat of nature. Building in a tropical environment is a difficult task: architectural challenges combine with breath-taking, yet demanding conditions. A successful tropical home not only provides protection from the elements, but also achieves a harmonious dialogue between people and their surroundings. The architects tackling such tasks are equally designers, landscape architects, and engineers; their works are symphonies in wood, stone, concrete, steel, and vegetation. This book takes you on a journey to the world's most fascinating tropical residential buildings. From the dense rainforests of South America to the idyllic islands of South East Asia, we present innovative residential projects that achieve a synergy between architecture and tropical vegetation. The buildings are consistently designed, sustainable masterpieces that skillfully showcase their interaction with nature. The lush, exotic vegetation becomes an integral element of the buildings' structure, flowing through the rooms, affording shade and fresh air, and giving the houses an organic vibrancy. The selected projects are characterized by the interplay of light and shadow, sophisticated use of natural ventilation, and the selection of materials that are smoothly embedded in the surroundings. As one explores the pages of this book, it is difficult to resist the charm of the fascinating tropical architecture it contains. May it not only serve as a source of inspiration to architects and designers, but also as an homage to the incomparable beauty and diversity of the tropics. The magic of their locations comes alive in these buildings...

CONTENT

CONTENT

FLOATING HOUSE

A

OTHER CREATIVES
Arquitetura Gui Mattos Interior Design
YEAR
2019
AREA
625.86 m²
NUMBER OF ROOMS
10
PHOTOGRAPHY
Carolina Lacaz, São Paulo

Built on a clearing in the Atlantic forest preceding the beach, the house floats slightly on its stone elements. The challenge was to insert the house into the natural topography and allow nature to take its course with minimal disruption. The search for diffused light resulted in the angular displacement of the roof slab, which runs the entire length of the house, as well as glass panels that open towards the path of the sun. In this way, the house enjoys plenty of natural light, ensuring a bright and vibrant atmosphere. The many openings frame the views into the forest. Wooden elements inserted into the concrete shell add comfort, warmth, and rhythm to the environment.

A Exterior view of the Floating House surrounded by nature
B View of the swimming pool overlooking the forest

B

C

C Bedroom with wooden ceiling
D Exterior view of the raised house
E View of the living area completely open to the terrace

D

E

F

G

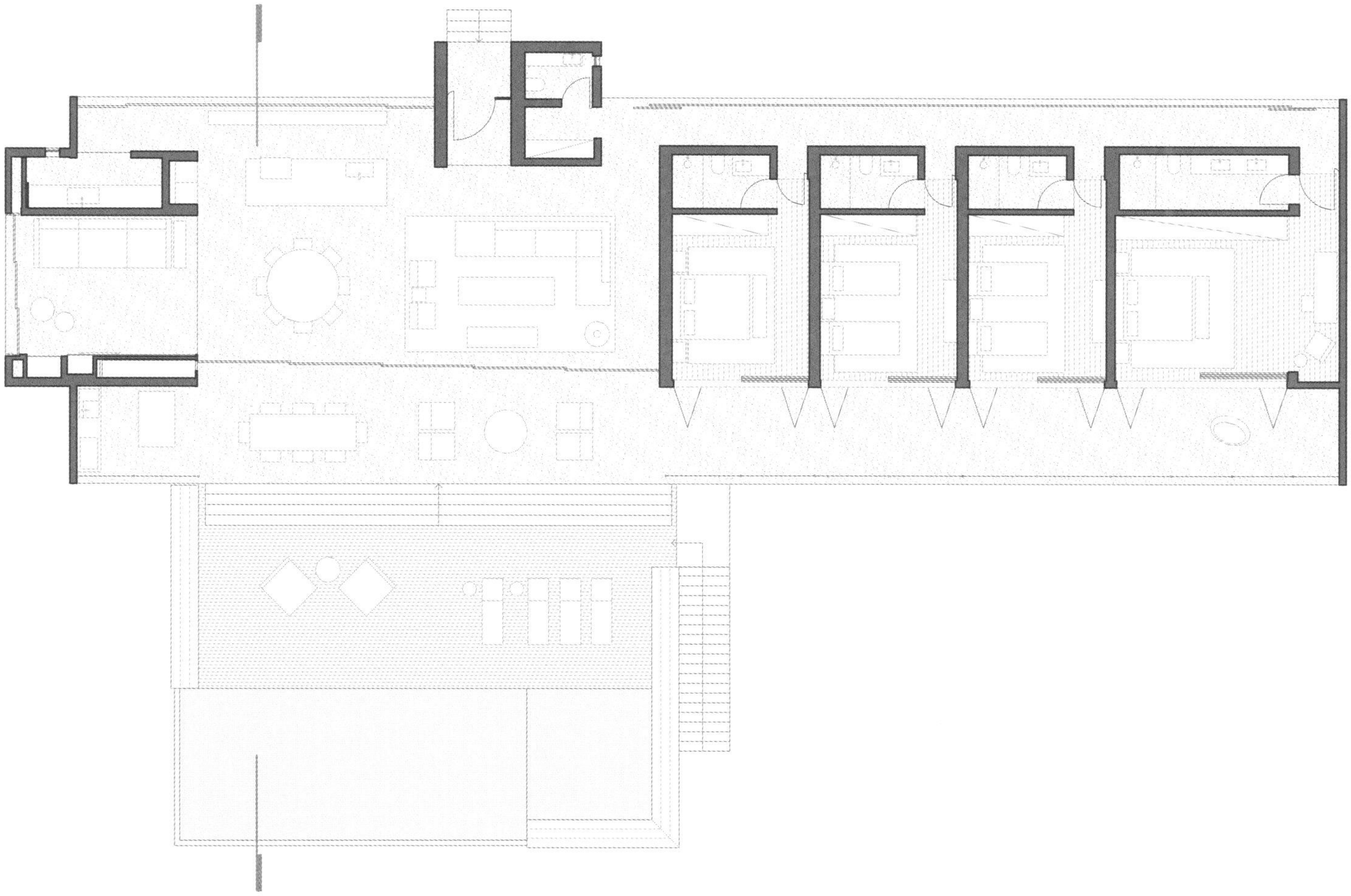

H

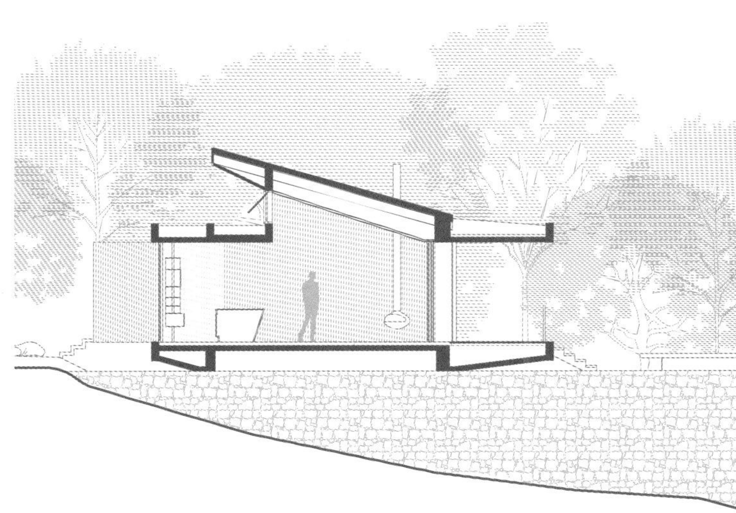

I

F View of the cozy sitting area open to the forest
G Front view of the main entrance
H First floor plan
I Cross section

CASA ACANTILADO

OTHER CREATIVES
Daniel Zozaya Valdes
Lead Architect,
Marusa Albarran
Interior Designer
YEAR
2021
AREA
777 m²
NUMBER OF ROOMS
4
FURTHER FACTS
Inspired by brutalism and modern Japanese architecture
PHOTOGRAPHY
Rafael Gamo

Situated on the cliffs of the Pacific coast of Guerrero, Casa Acantilado is surrounded by unique vegetation, while various bird species nest on the rock face. The main volume is based on two slightly rotated geometrical elements that guide one's view towards the Pacific. The topography was the defining factor for this project's spatial organization. Entering the building directly from the upper floor, one is greeted by a large palapa accommodating the house's social areas. The palapa was made by local craftsmen using regional materials such as stone, wood, and palm leaves. Its form uses the natural light and cross-ventilation to reduce energy consumption. An infinity pool partially connected to the main structure links the building to the Pacific. The stairs to the private area lead past concrete walls that allow one to sense the exterior environment, while remaining shielded. The lobby leads to rooms that all have their own private terraces, which open out towards the incredible landscape.

A Main view of Casa Acantilado surrounded by natural landscape
B Living and dining area overlooking the ocean

B

C D

E

F

G

C Interior view of the kitchen.
D Cozy living area with curved sofa surrounded by nature
E Bedroom open to the terrace with panoramic view
F Outdoor terrace with infinity pool overlooking the ocean
G Private pool

H

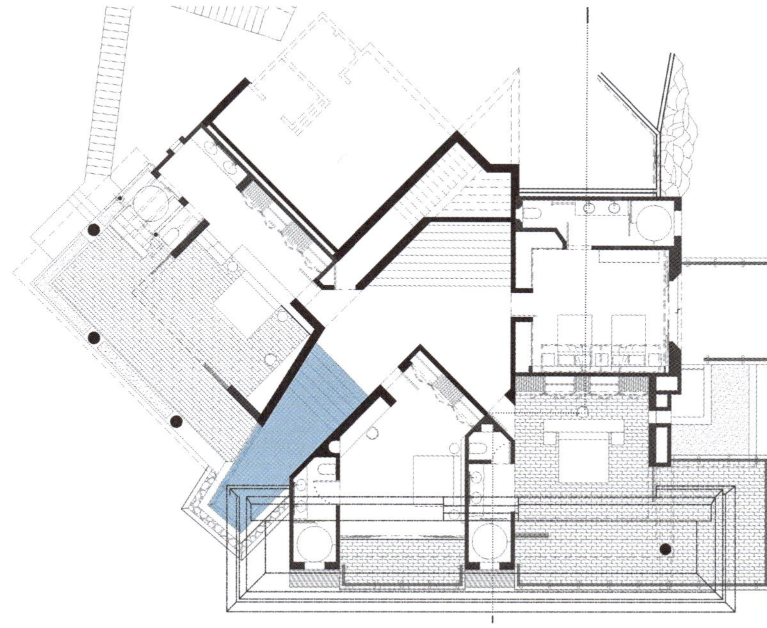

I

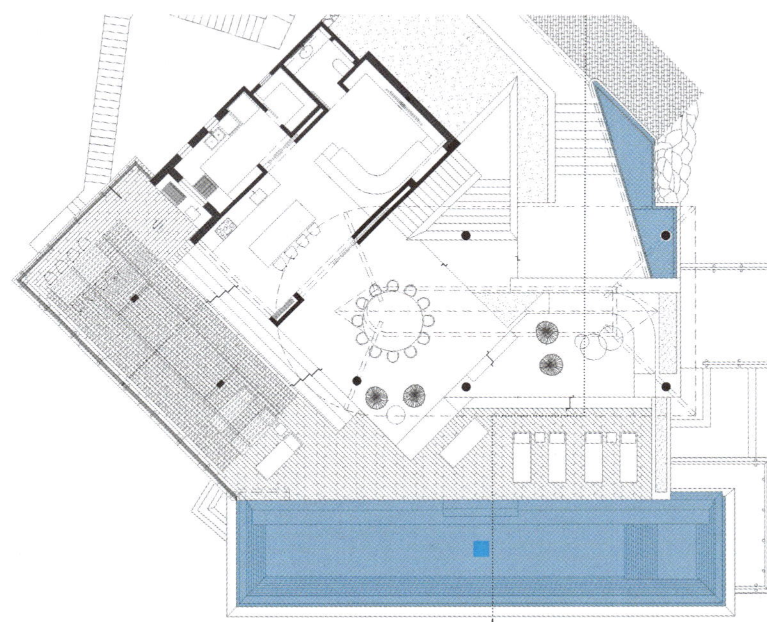

J

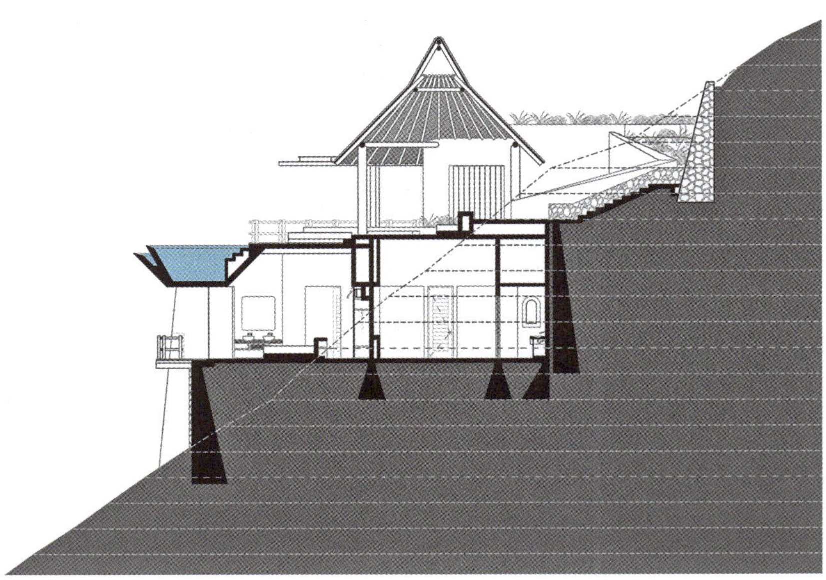

K

H View of the infinity pool suspended over the ocean
I First floor plan
J Second floor plan
K Section

20

VALENTINA AUDRITO
STUDIO AUDRITO

CHAMELEON VILLA

YEAR
2017
AREA
1,015 m^2
NUMBER OF ROOMS
6
FURTHER FACTS
Built on a steep slope overlooking the river
PHOTOGRAPHY
Moch Sulthonn for Studio Audrito

The Chameleon Villa in Buwit, Bali, covers a acre of land and affords breath-taking views of the forest and river. The challenge was to create architecture that could be seamlessly integrated into the topography of the steep terrain. The "landscape architecture" blurs the boundaries between nature and building, making the structures appear to be part of the natural environment. Situated on various terrain levels, the buildings are perfectly integrated into the surroundings, providing unique vantage points. The pavilions serve various functions and are inspired by traditional Balinese architecture. Communal rooms are open, while more private units can be closed off. The development conjures an atmosphere of discovery: Unexpected and surprising solutions are revealed as one progresses through the building, beginning with the car park and ending in the guest rooms on a lower level. "Camouflaged" roofs cool the rooms and collect rainwater, while technical equipment is stored beneath them.

A View of the guest's bathroom patio from above
B The dining area with built-in seating overlooking the pool

B

C Exterior view of the plant-covered façade from the terrace with infinity pool

C

D E

F

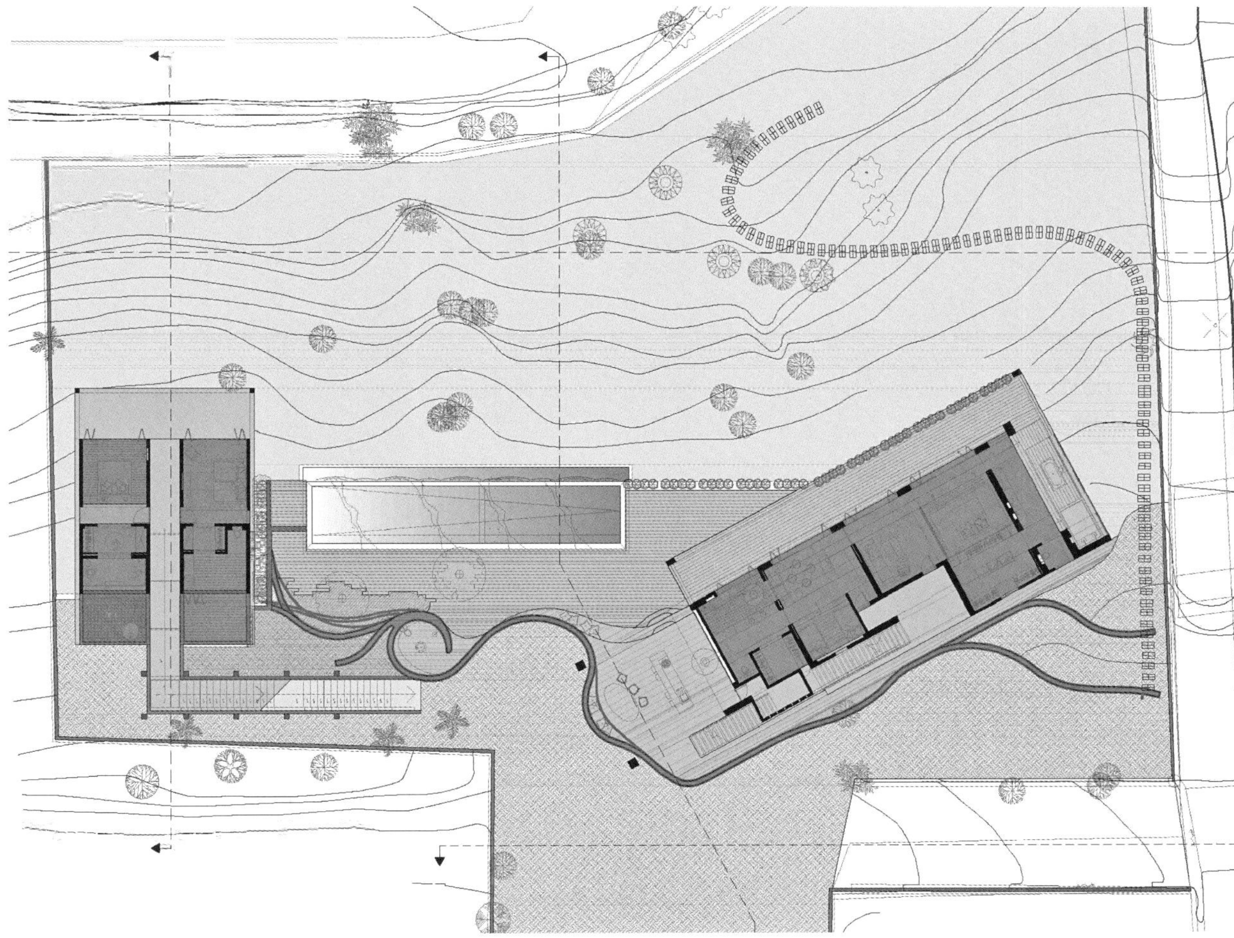

G

D One bedroom with panoramic view of the surrounding nature
E Master bathroom with floor bath
F Interior view of the main living area
G Site plan

CALA SAONA

A

OTHER CREATIVES
Landscape and Interior Design by BIOMBO ARCHITECTS
YEAR
2019
AREA
650 m^2
NUMBER OF ROOMS
8
FURTHER FACTS
Oasis beach pool surrounded by tropical coconut trees
PHOTOGRAPHY
KIEARCH

Designed by Biombo Architects, this family retreat is situated in Canggu, Bali. It consists of the main, five-bedroom "Cala Saona" and a three-bedroom guest pavilion housing the "Batukaru Suites". Both sections have their own pool and terrace. The sections can be used as two separate units or as a single villa with eight bedrooms, making them ideal as a family residence or for rental. Oriented toward the sunset and surrounded by rice fields, the residence is a breathtaking oasis of peace. "Cala Saona" impresses with a tropical inner garden, a 17-meter-long marble pool, and a generous living area on the ground floor. The covered terraces and the pool zone are perfect for enjoying the sunset. Three bedrooms with private bathrooms and an outdoor terrace are situated on the upper level. The multifunctional room in the basement provides space and additional storage capacity. The "Batukaru Suites" supplement the property with three additional suites, each with a glass pool and a view of the rice fields. The elegant residence combines luxury and the natural beauty of Bali.

A View of Cala Saona from the pool
B View of the interior space open to the garden

B

C

D

E

F

- C Interior view of the double-height living room with the cozy sofa area
- D Dining and living area open to garden
- E View of one bedroom
- F Exterior view of the house in the evening

G Interior details
H Main façade overlooking the swimming pool
I First floor plan
J Longitudinal section

G

H

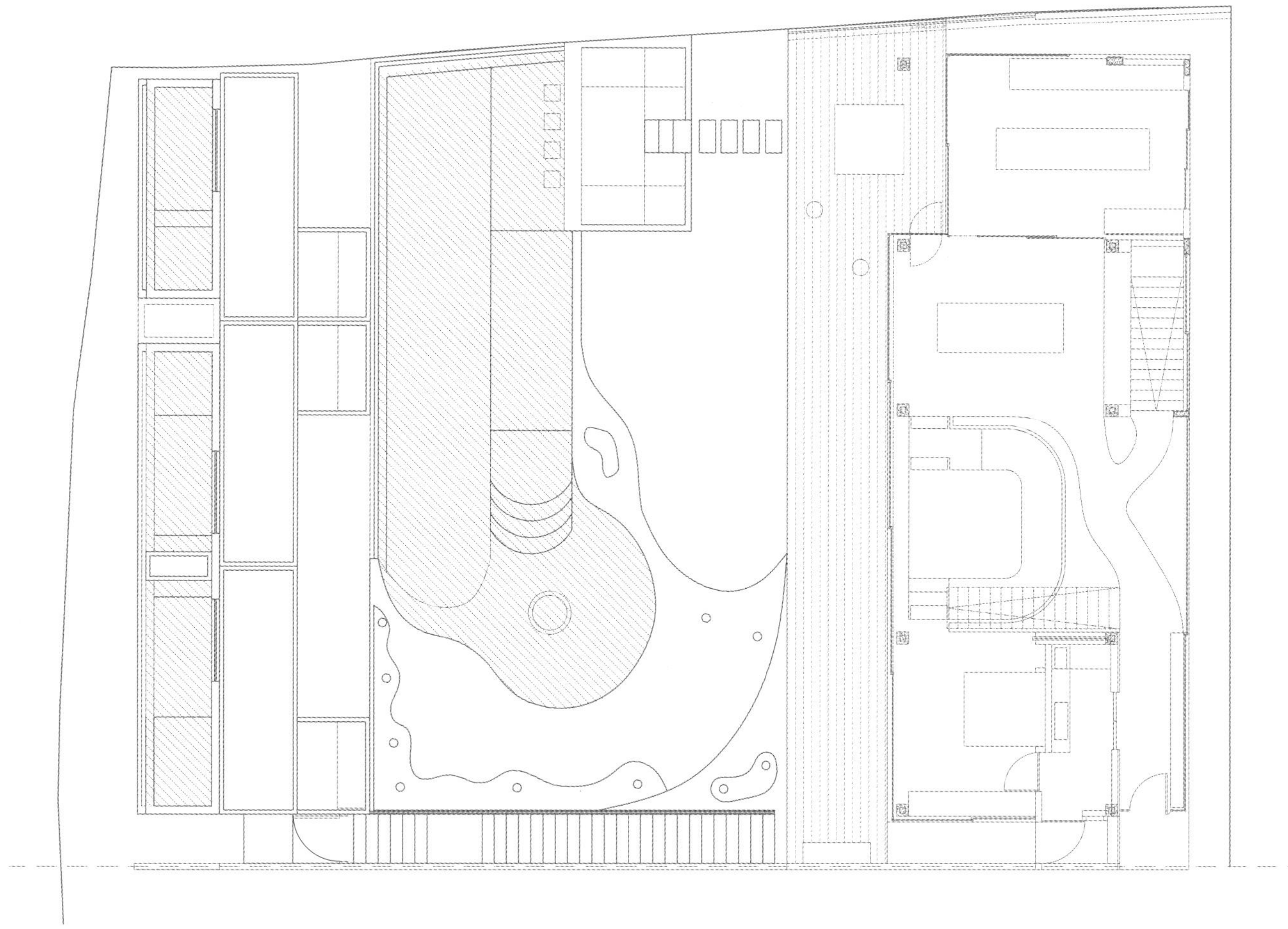

I

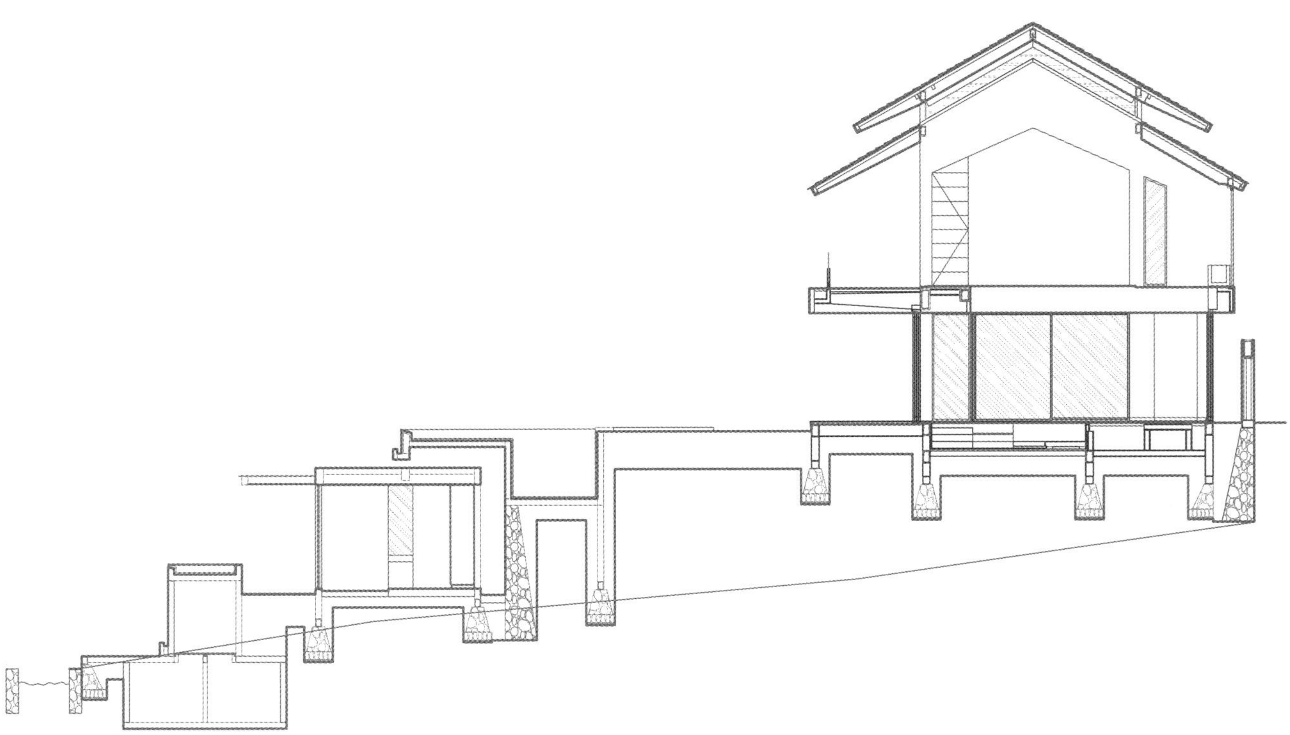

J

THE TERRACE APARTMENT

OTHER CREATIVES
Juliana Freitas landscape, Foco Luz e Desenho lighting, Harmonia Acústica acoustic, Noise automation, I2N air conditioning and hydraulic design, Juntxs. Lab lighting audio reactive

YEAR
2022

AREA
280 m²

NUMBER OF ROOMS
4

PHOTOGRAPHY
Maíra Acayaba

Combining tradition and modernity, the Terrace Apartment in São Paulo is an innovative example of hybrid architecture. Designed by Guto Requena, it transforms an architectural icon conceived in 1962 into a flexible, reconfigurable residential environment. Concrete and digital technology, including automated, intelligent controls, provide the apartment with diverse, adaptable uses. Sliding acoustic-glass doors and automatic curtains create flexible rooms that can be integrated or isolated as required. The kitchen is versatile and can be transformed into a home cinema, a conference room, or a dance floor. The broad terrace's lush vegetation offers an urban forest with fruit trees and a large vegetable garden. The design focuses on flexibility and adaptability. The façade also combines collective and intimate zones, making it an example of hybrid parametric design. The project is the result of Guto Requenas's 20-year study of the effects of digital technologies on architecture and design: an example of modern, flexible living in the digital age.

A View of the living area of The Terrace Appartment
B Exterior view of the façade with shutters
C View from the dining area

B C

D

E

D View of the bedroom
E Detail of the bathroom with a plant-covered window
F View of the cozy living room with several plants

G

G Detail of the steel and wood kitchen with cooking island
H Bookcase hiding sliding walls that separate the different rooms

H

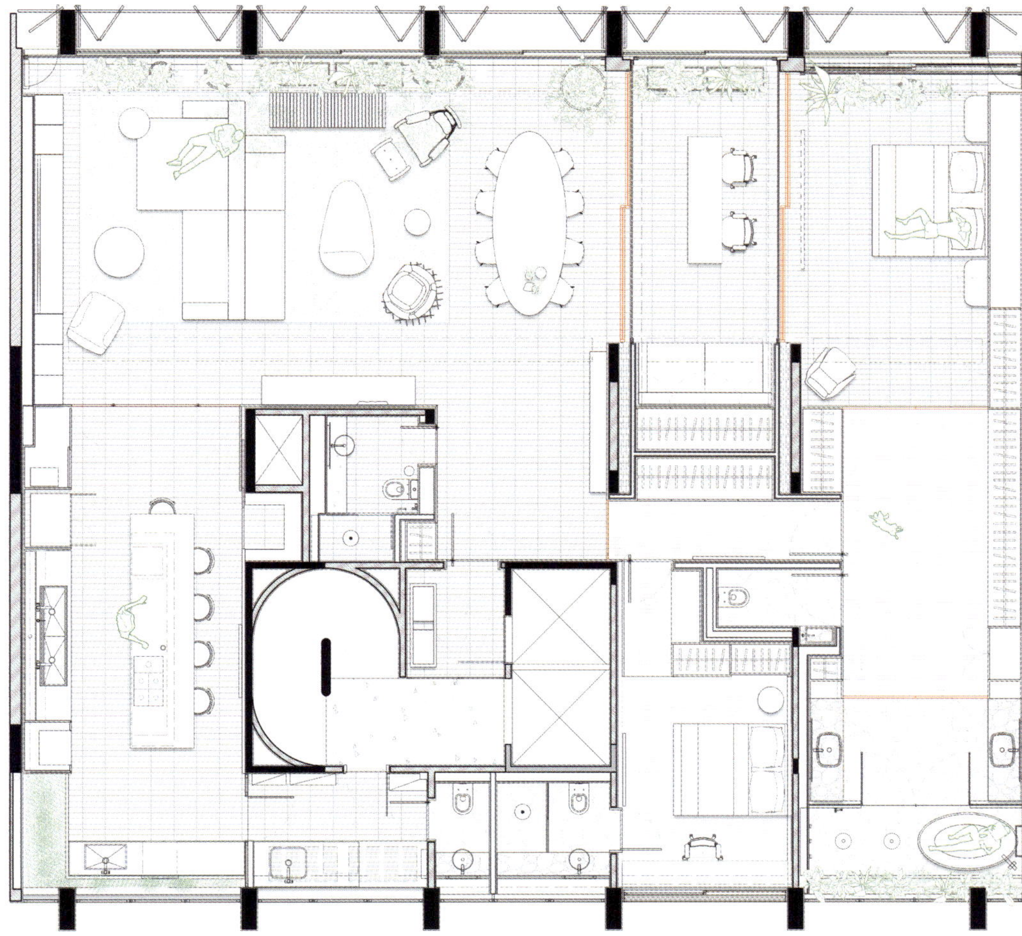

I

I Floor plan of The Terrace Apartment with movable walls that make the space completely flexible

LA EXTRAVIADA

A

OTHER CREATIVES
Gala Sánchez-Renero
Interior Design
YEAR
2020
AREA
472 m^2
NUMBER OF
ROOMS
4
PHOTOGRAPHY
Emanuel Velasquez,
Nin Solis and Diego
Padilla Magallanes

"La Extraviada is a fish that turned into a dream that turned into a project that turned into a house overlooking the sea." With its view of the Pacific Ocean, La Extraviada was built on a hill above the peaceful, majestic Mermejita beach, completely surrounded by nature. La Extraviada is a project for holidays in Mazunte, Oaxaca, where it is always hot. The house was developed with this in mind, using the natural forces it faces, rather than resisting them. The climate, salt, sun, and humidity are key design elements. The house is nestled into the hillside and merges with the topography. Its geometry creates overlapping volumes resembling stacked stones with large wooden windows. Adaptation to the terrain produces patios and canopies that provide shade and allow the breeze to pass through. The concrete used throughout the project allows the architecture's construction on such a steep slope, making it an ideal canvas that changes over time together with the countryside.

A Aerial view of La Extraviada
B Interior view of the dining room and kitchen

B

C

D

C The cozy living room open to the garden
D Exterior view of the cantilever volumes
E View of the pool overlooking the sea from the veranda
F The Extraviada from the garden

E

F

G

G Interior view of one bedroom with cozy balcony
H Exterior view of the house surrounded by nature
I Floor plan of the independent studio
J Floor plan of the social area

H

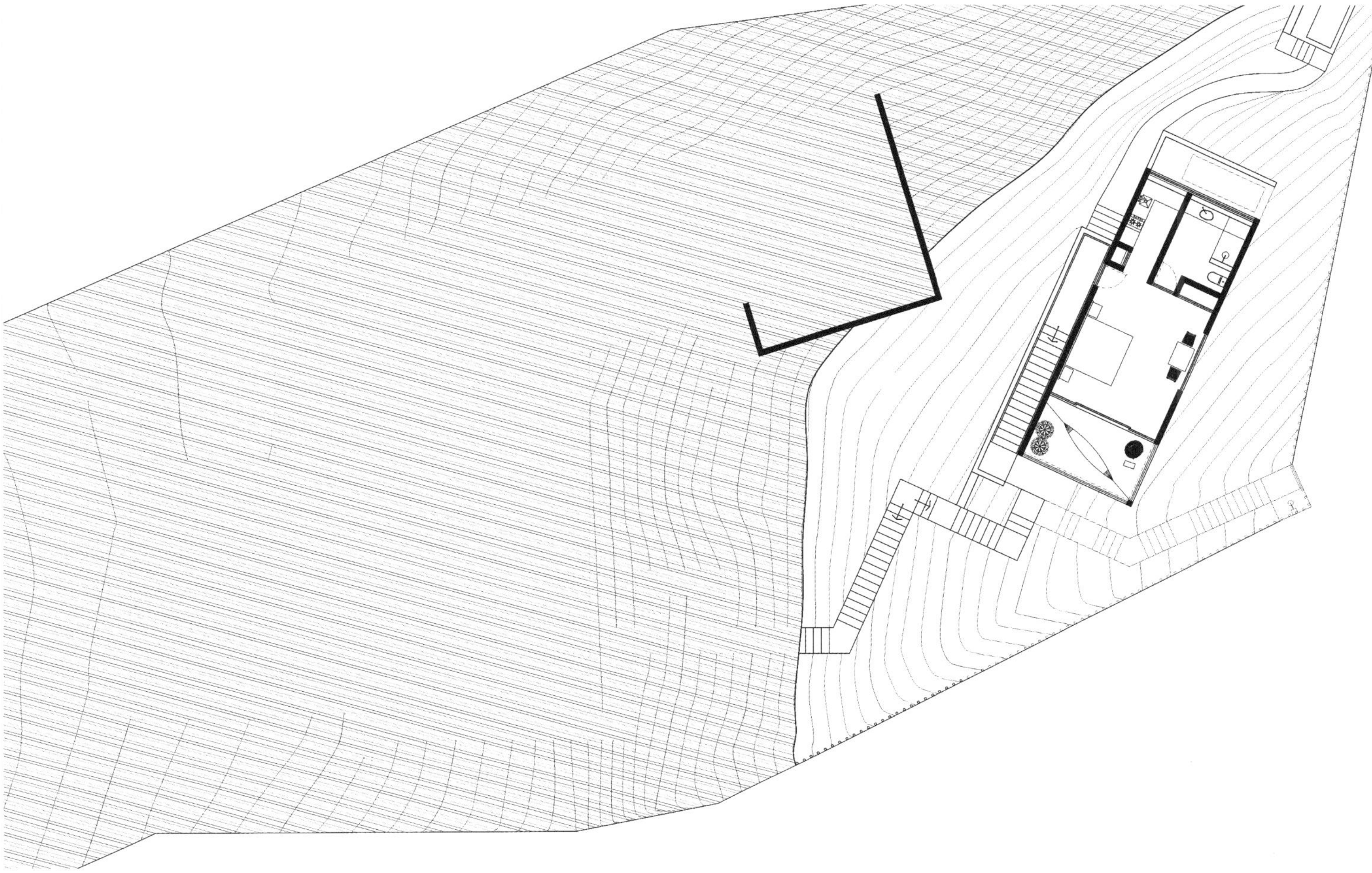

I

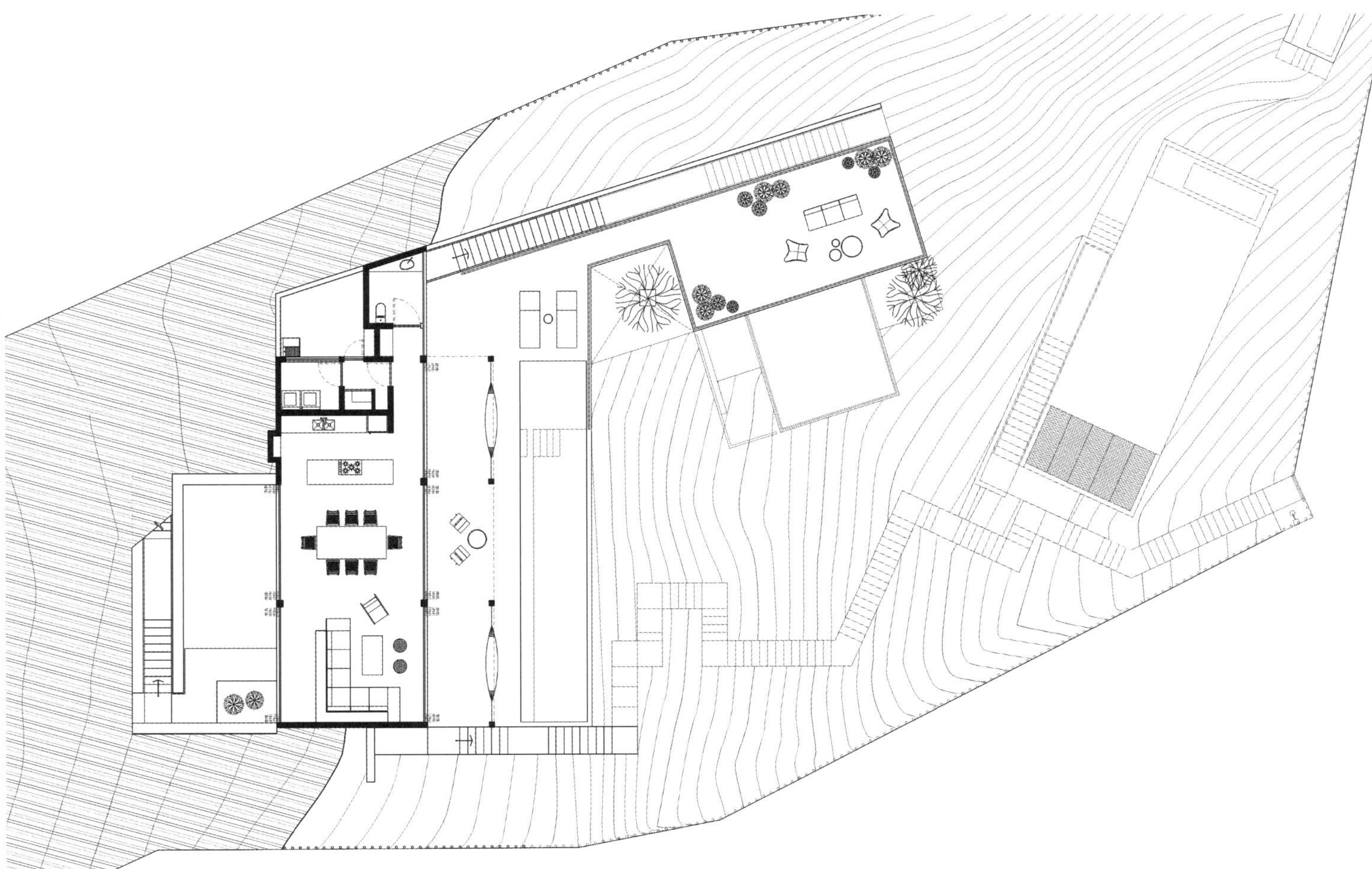

J

PARIKRAMA HOUSE

A

YEAR
2020
AREA
750 m²
NUMBER OF ROOMS
4
PHOTOGRAPHY
Umang Shah, India

A remarkable house stands amid a lush coconut grove in the region of Murud, combining perfect modern architecture with ecological sustainability. The building is set in the surrounding greenery, its impressive windows allowing interior and exterior spaces to merge. The architecture arranges the bedrooms in a row, while the main living and dining areas are elevated at opposite building ends. This design achieves a sense of a "Parikrama" or circuit around the building, as residents remain in constant contact with the surrounding nature. The house's main materials are robust tilt-up stone slabs consisting of 40-millimeter-thick granite, an extremely sustainable material with very few environmental impacts, from being quarried to its processing on the building site. The combination of glass panels and massive stone slabs gives the house a modern appearance during the day, while offering a magical interplay of light at night. The building exudes durability and reminds us that, in a changing world, materials such as stone will always remain.

A Main view of Parikrama House
B Interior view of the dining room overlooking the garden

B

C View of the house surrounded by palm trees at sunset

C

D E

F

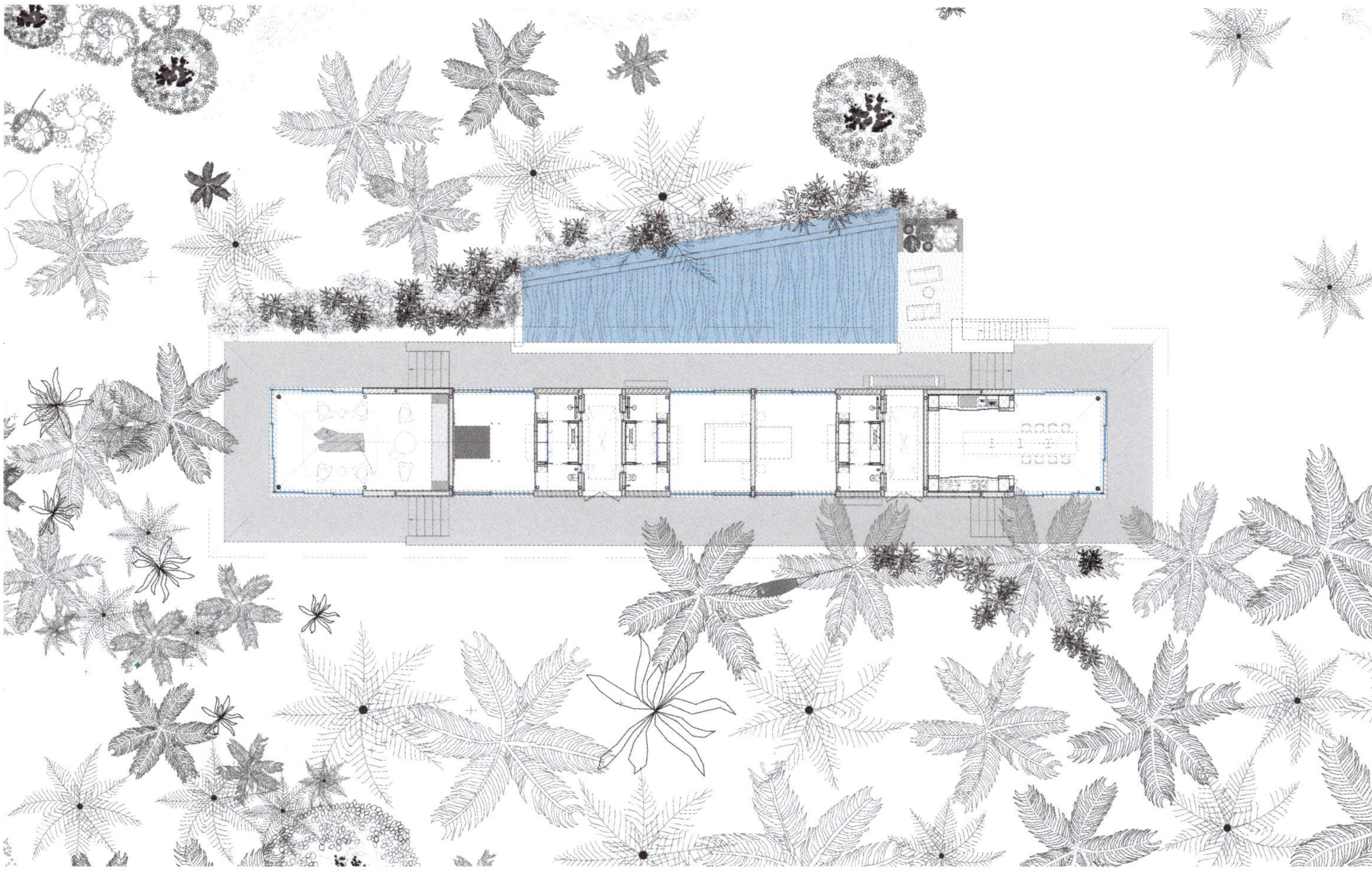

G

D The pool borders the granite body of the veranda
E Interior view of one bedroom open to the garden
F Side view of Parikrama House
G Floor plan

CASA PATIO

YEAR
2019
AREA
800 m²
NUMBER OF ROOMS
11
FURTHER FACTS
Contemporary tropical design
PHOTOGRAPHY
Andrés García, Putarenas Costa Rica

Casa Patio is situated in Playa Herradura, a luxury residential community in Puntarenas, Costa Rica. The building is surrounded by lush gardens and offers a captivating view of the Pacific Ocean. The flat property is flanked by gentle hills. Extended over 800 square meters, the house consists of a main volume for private zones and a transversal block for auxiliary areas, which seamlessly merges with the terrace and the central patio. The building's alignment was chosen to focus on the wonderful view of the sea and the sunsets. In addition to service areas, the house accommodates five bedrooms and a master bedroom. The central patio interleaves the indoor and outdoor spaces, thereby providing a very comfortable atmosphere for living with and in the green environment. The design combines modern architecture with a sustainable handling of the local climate and the Costa Rican surroundings.

A Main view of the patio
B Front view of the entrance of Casa Patio

B

F

C Terrace with infinity pool at sunset
D Living area on the main terrace
E Exterior view of the back façade and swimming pool at sunset
F View of the living and dining room from the patio

G

H

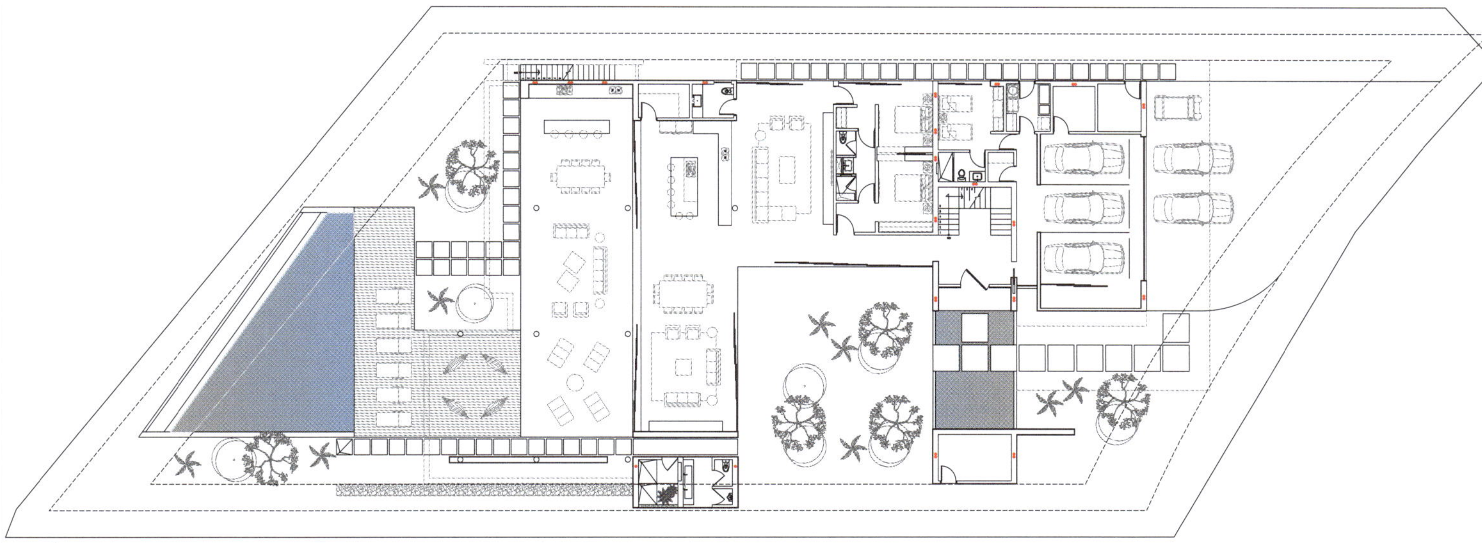

I

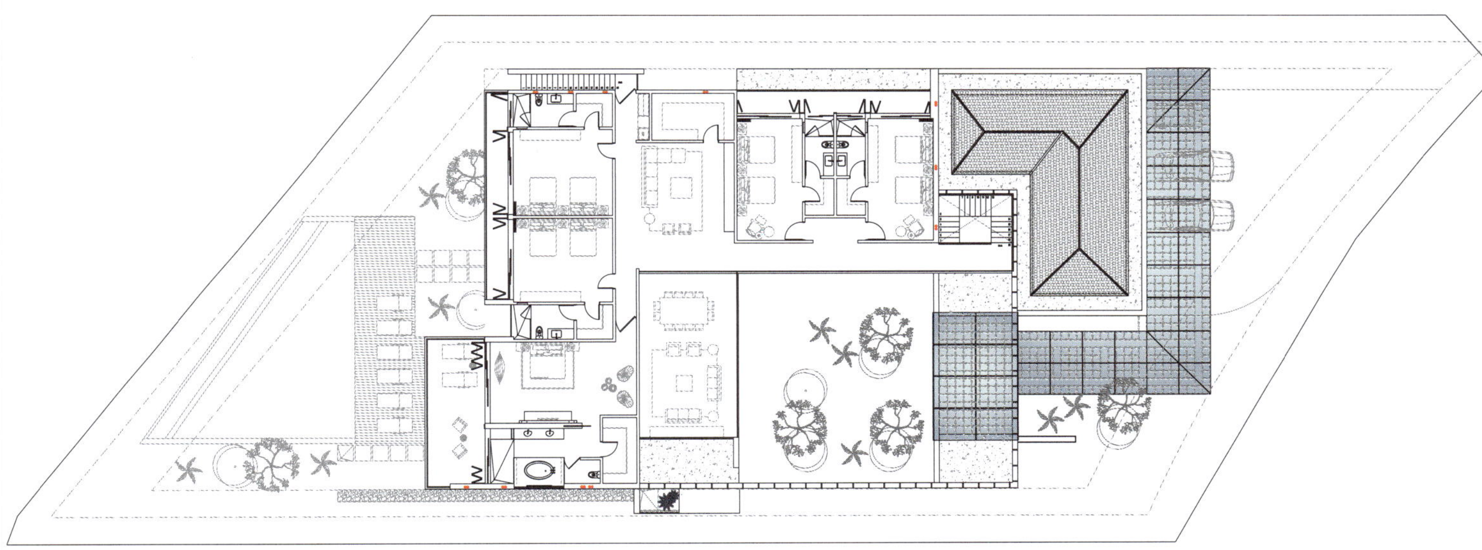

J

G Main view of Casa Patio
H Detail of the perforated wooden canopy in the entrance area
I First floor plan
J Second floor plan

HOUSE Q04L63

A

OTHER CREATIVES
Filipi Oliveira, Mariana Oliveira, Luis Fernando, Luis Felipe, Lucas Ferrari, Talita Faciroli, Guilherme Takahashi, Renato Ubiali and Dionésio Júnior
YEAR
2020
AREA
282 m²
NUMBER OF ROOMS
6
PHOTOGRAPHY
Felipe Araújo

House Q04L63 is a summer residence for a married couple with three children. The design allocated 50 percent of the space to social interaction, in areas such as the dining room, living room, swimming pool, and steam bath. The remaining space accommodates more intimate areas for all family members. The introverted zone is placed in the front section of the building and separated from the rear by a central hallway. Natural materials such as travertine marble from Egypt, black slate, rustic granite, concrete slabs, and hijau stones were chosen as cladding to create an inviting, timeless space. The skillfully placed apertures and high-quality details create a secluded, yet open atmosphere. Wood and carefully selected furniture by designers such as Jader Almeida, Paulo Alves, and Martin Eisler follow a uniform color and formal scheme. The house is harmoniously embedded into the riverside environment, while the vegetation blends in with the surroundings. The simple, functional design offers a comfortable, functional residence for all visitors.

A Exterior view of House Q04L63 at sunset
B The main entrance

B

C The covered entrance area
D Interior view of the living area
E The terrace with swimming pool from the living area
F Detail of the lamellar roofing
G The living area with open dining and kitchen area

C

D

E

F G

H

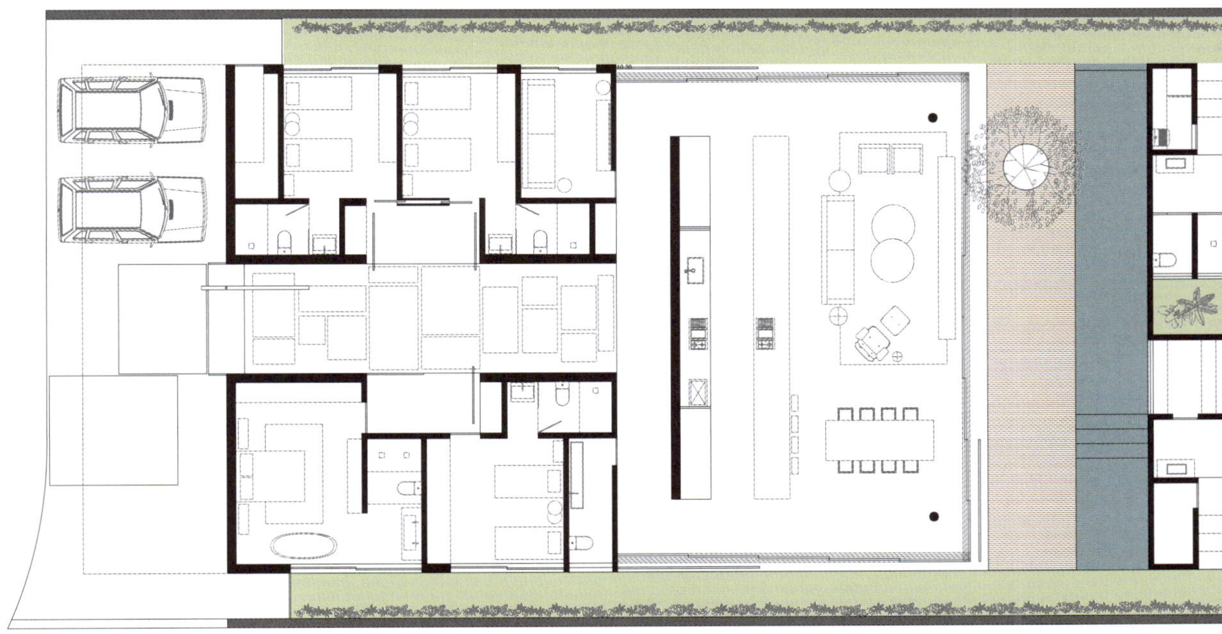

I

H View of the covered entrance hallway
I Floor plan

DHSAC RESIDENCE

A

OTHER CREATIVES
Agatha Carolina
architect and
interior designer
YEAR
2022
AREA
450 m^2
NUMBER OF
ROOMS
3
PHOTOGRAPHY
Ernest Theofilus

Agatha Carolina regards her home not only as a retreat, but also as a place of growth and aging together. The Dhsac Residence, the first home she has designed for the family, unites modern mid-century design with adaptations to the tropical surroundings. Large apertures, long roofs, and natural materials create an airy space with good lighting conditions. The two-story house consists of two volumes that meet at an angle of 90 degrees. The large openings reveal the inner courtyard, while reflecting pools and louvers modulate the light. The Dhsac Residence is a loving manifestation of Agatha's dedication to her growing family.

A View of Dhsac Residence
B Interior view of the double-height living room
C The dining area overlooking the garden

B C

D

E

F

G

D View of the terrace from the garden
E Main bathroom with an outdoor bathing area
F Interior view of one bedroom
G Work area on the second floor overlooking the living room

H Interior view of the kitchen
I View from the garden of Dhsac Residence at sunset

H

I

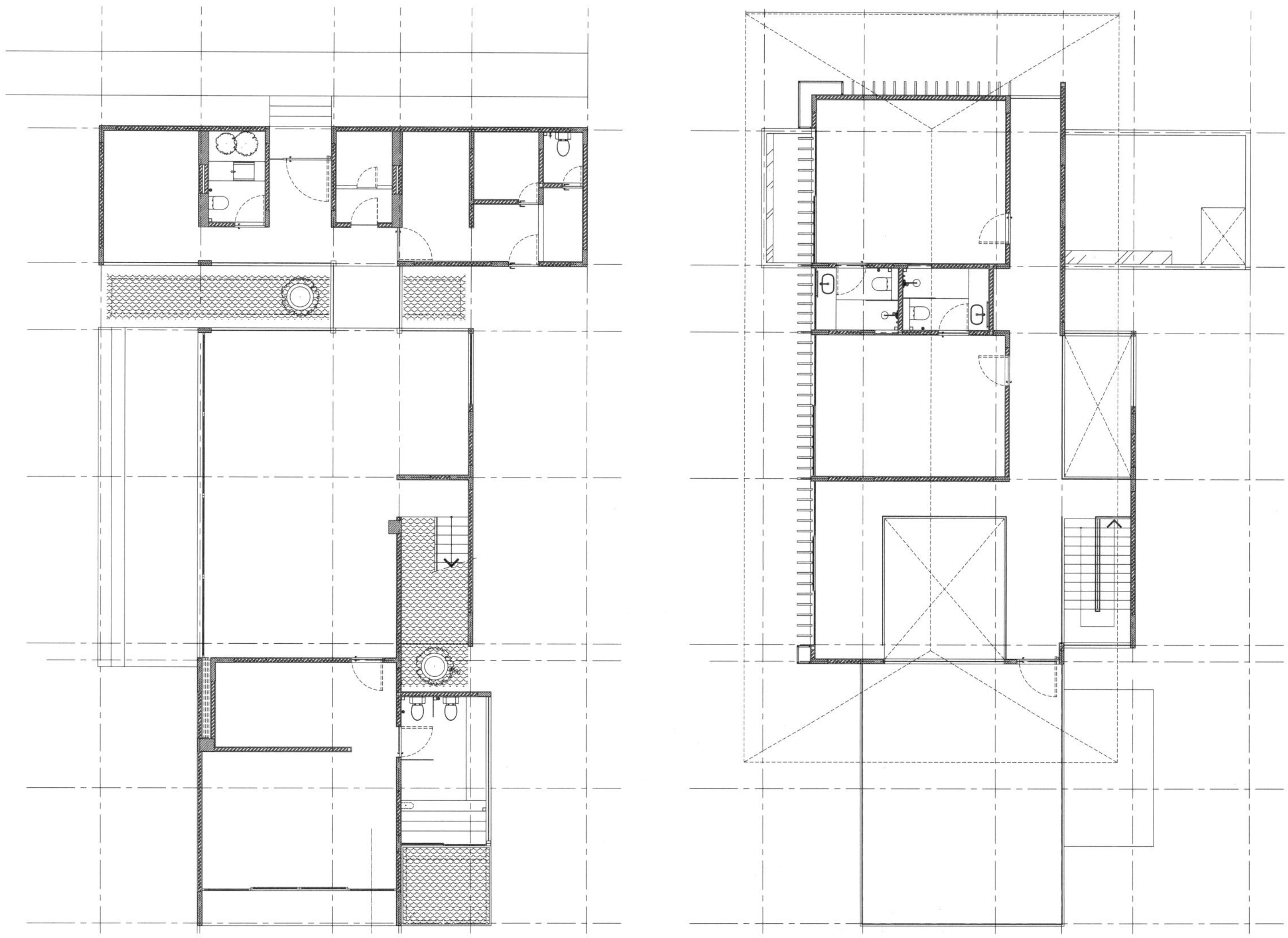

J K

J First floor plan
K Second floor plan

MLT HOUSE

A

OTHER CREATIVES
Lightworks and Cenário Paisagismo Landscape
YEAR
2020
AREA
469.63 m^2
NUMBER OF ROOMS
12
FURTHER FACTS
Looking for a unique identity, some of the furniture pieces and house details were designed by Bernardes' team
PHOTOGRAPHY
Leonardo Finotti

This holiday retreat in Mata de São João, Bahia offers its residents privacy, while allowing them to enjoy the spectacular countryside. The architecture consists of two independent brick volumes arranged on a trapezoid slab. The larger volume accommodates the service areas, while the auxiliary rooms are in the smaller volume. A central, open zone connects the living room to the dining room, offering a marvelous view of the beach. The open façade transforms the living room into a large patio. The upper level accommodates the private areas and a studio. The balconies and suites have a staggered arrangement, inwardly guiding the airflow and natural light. The façades offer a balance between transparency and seclusion. The butterfly roof guides rainwater into a storage tank for reuse, while adding lightness to the architecture. Natural materials such as wood and local stones were chosen for the outdoor facilities, to achieve a harmonious connection to the green landscape. Inside, Bahian atmospheres are reinterpreted to produce contemporary solutions.

A Exterior view of MLT House
B Cozy balcony with hammock overlooking the garden

B

C Main view of the house from the garden with swimming pool

C

D E

F

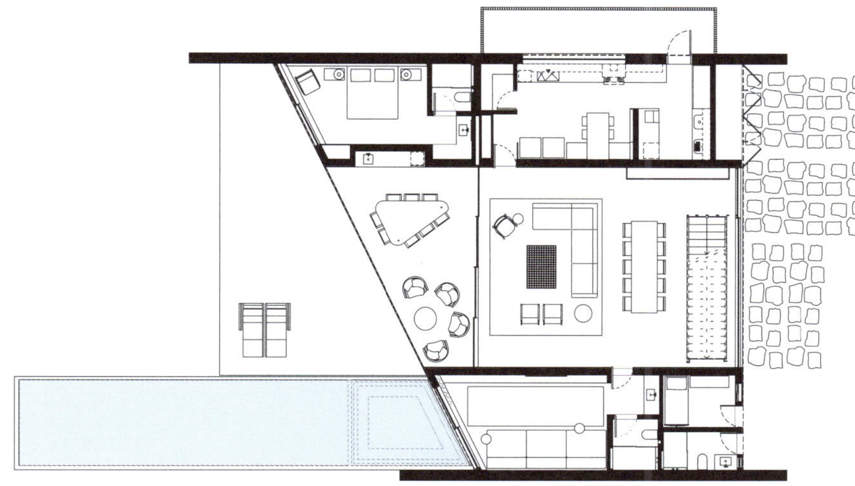

G

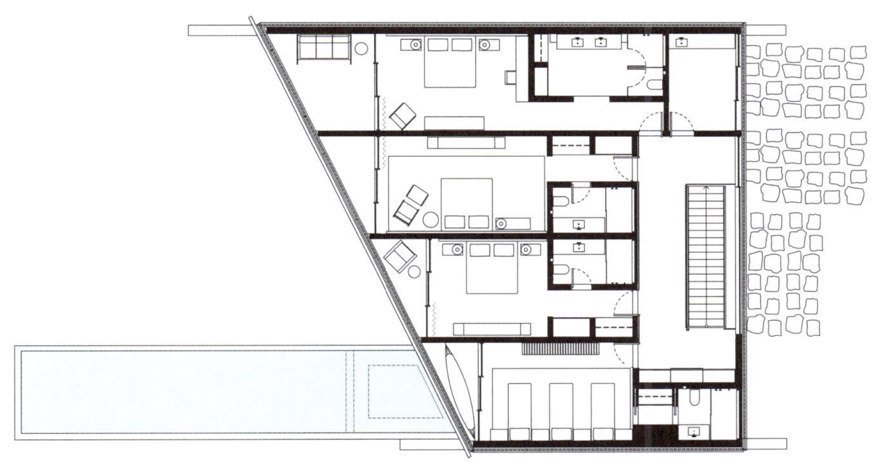

H

D Front view of the stone and perforated wood façade
E The pool overlooking the sea
F View of the living room
G First floor plan
H Second floor plan

VENICE BEACH HOUSE

A

OTHER CREATIVES
The Office of Gordon L. Polon Structural Engineer, Oculus Light Studio, Wynn Engineering, Bent Grass Landscape Design
YEAR
2019
AREA
523 m²
NUMBER OF ROOMS
4
PHOTOGRAPHY
Kevin Scott

A Exterior view of Venice Beach House
B View of the exterior garden marking the interior spaces

Completed in 2019, the house was designed around three outdoor areas that provide additional space for living in the southern Californian climate. The large garden area is used as an extension of the reception zone, while two smaller gardens are integrated into the floor plan to enable more private moments and views along the ground floor. The house in the Venice Beach seaside neighborhood was conceived for a family and combines industrial elements such as concrete-block walls and polished floors with the warmth of wood. Powder-coated window elements, black steel frames, and metal cladding evoke a mid-century materiality and achieve an overall spatial experience. The vegetation creates an intimate ground-floor area that smoothly merges with the garden. The light, wooden-clad upper level and the separate pool building become autonomous pavilions. Black walls made of standard masonry units are arranged in parallel both inside and outdoors, forming the central structures. They create a unity between the garden and the reception zone. The floor plan ensures that all principal rooms have their own outdoor spaces, thereby extending the sight lines, maximizing the spatial perception, and ensuring good natural lighting.

B

C

D

C Main view of the house
D Interior staircase with natural and warm wood tones
E View of the living room entirely open to the garden

F G

H

I

F Interior view
G Dining and kitchen area
H View of the living room with sliding glass doors leading to the garden
I Longitudinal section

MHS HOUSE

YEAR
2016
AREA
135 m²
NUMBER OF ROOMS
3
PHOTOGRAPHY
SKY|GROUND

MHS House in Mae Hong Son, Thailand, was designed by ASWA, Architectural Studio of Work - Aholic, for a German-Thai couple. Inspired by the surrounding mountain landscape, the building consists of three interlocking concrete volumes that form a sculptural ensemble. Each volume has dimensions of 6.60 x 6.60 meters and a height of 3.45 meters. Inside, the ground floor provides a spacious living zone, a pantry, and a rest room. The second floor accommodates an office and the covered terrace, as well as a jacuzzi. The bedrooms are aligned to highlight the beautiful surrounding mountains through the generous, room-high windows. The façades are made of cement on the base level, while presenting a wooden material on the upper levels – exuding a sense of security and stability, while also expressing lightness. Natural ventilation and solar energy on the roof ensure a high level of energy efficiency. The 135 square meters floor space successfully combines well-integrated modern design and sustainable construction.

A Exterior view at twilight
B View of the surrounding nature from the balcony with hammock

B

C Side view of MHS House from the garden

C

D Central open stairwell
E Main view of the sculpturally shaped house

D

E

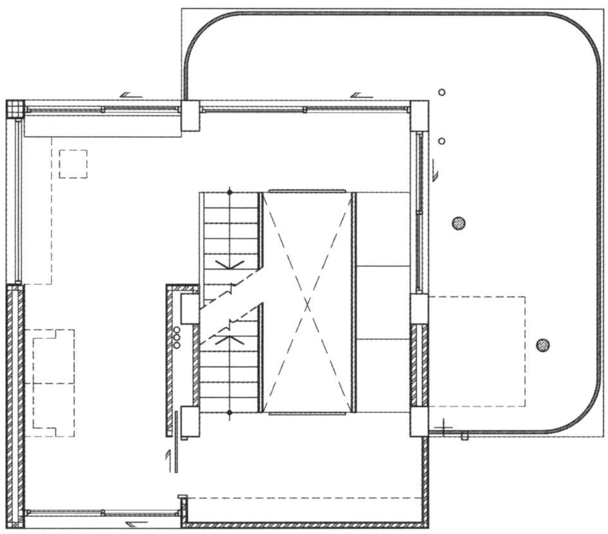

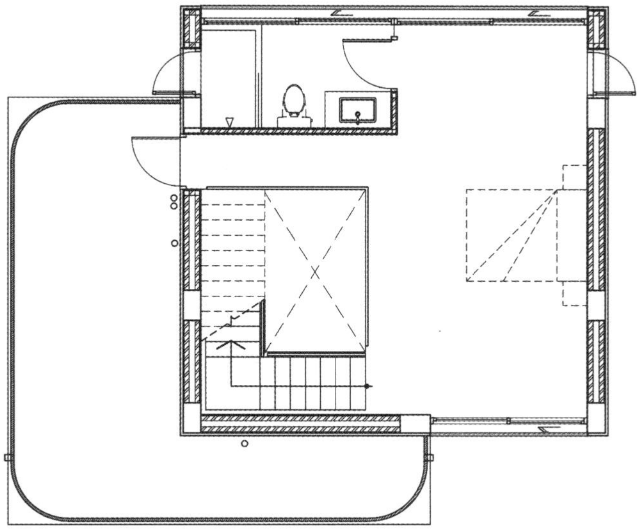

F G

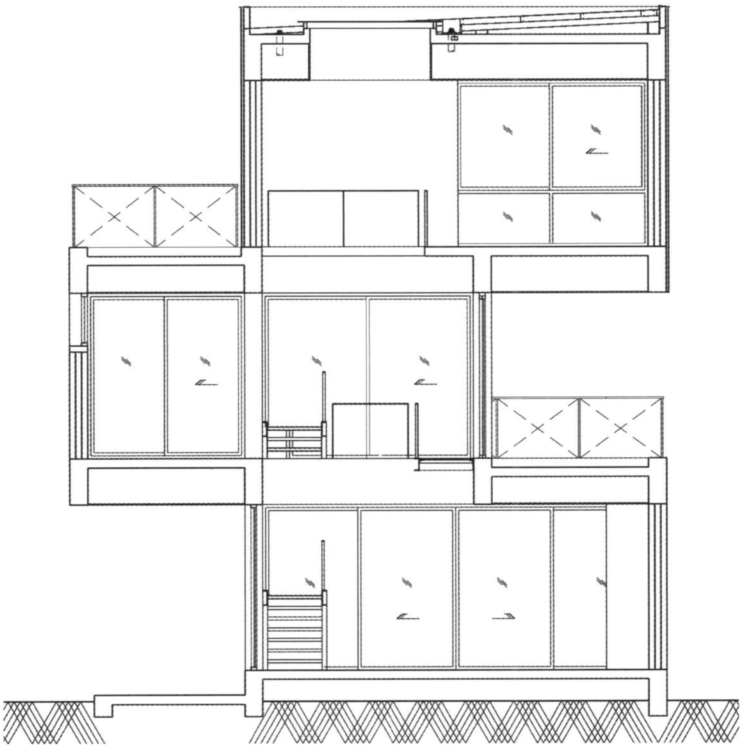

F Second floor plan
G Third floor plan
H Section

H

ME ARQUITETURA

LOFT RLO

YEAR
2020
AREA
250 m^2
NUMBER OF ROOMS
2
FURTHER FACTS
Interior design and custom-built cabinetry by ME Arquitetura
PHOTOGRAPHY
Haruo Mikami

ME Arquitetura has designed a pavilion that inherently captures and supports an outdoor lifestyle. A single-story home with generous proportions merges the boundaries between indoor and outdoor worlds to strengthen the ground-floor experience and make the symbiosis between residential and non-residential zones tangible. The reduced palette of natural materials underlines the connection to the garden and the lake, while highlighting the project's linear geometry. The room-high glass doors slide into the the wooden slats behind the kitchen, creating a single space that accommodates the dining room, kitchen, veranda, and pool deck. The rectilinear house refers to the natural environment by creating visual perspectives that showcase the lakefront.

A Main view of Loft RLO from the garden
B Lakefront view from the covered terrace

B

C D

E

F

G

C Kitchen and dining room
D Main bathroom with large window overlooking the garden
E Side view of the outdoor living area overlooking the pool and the garden
F Bedroom open to the terrace
G Interior view of the living area

H

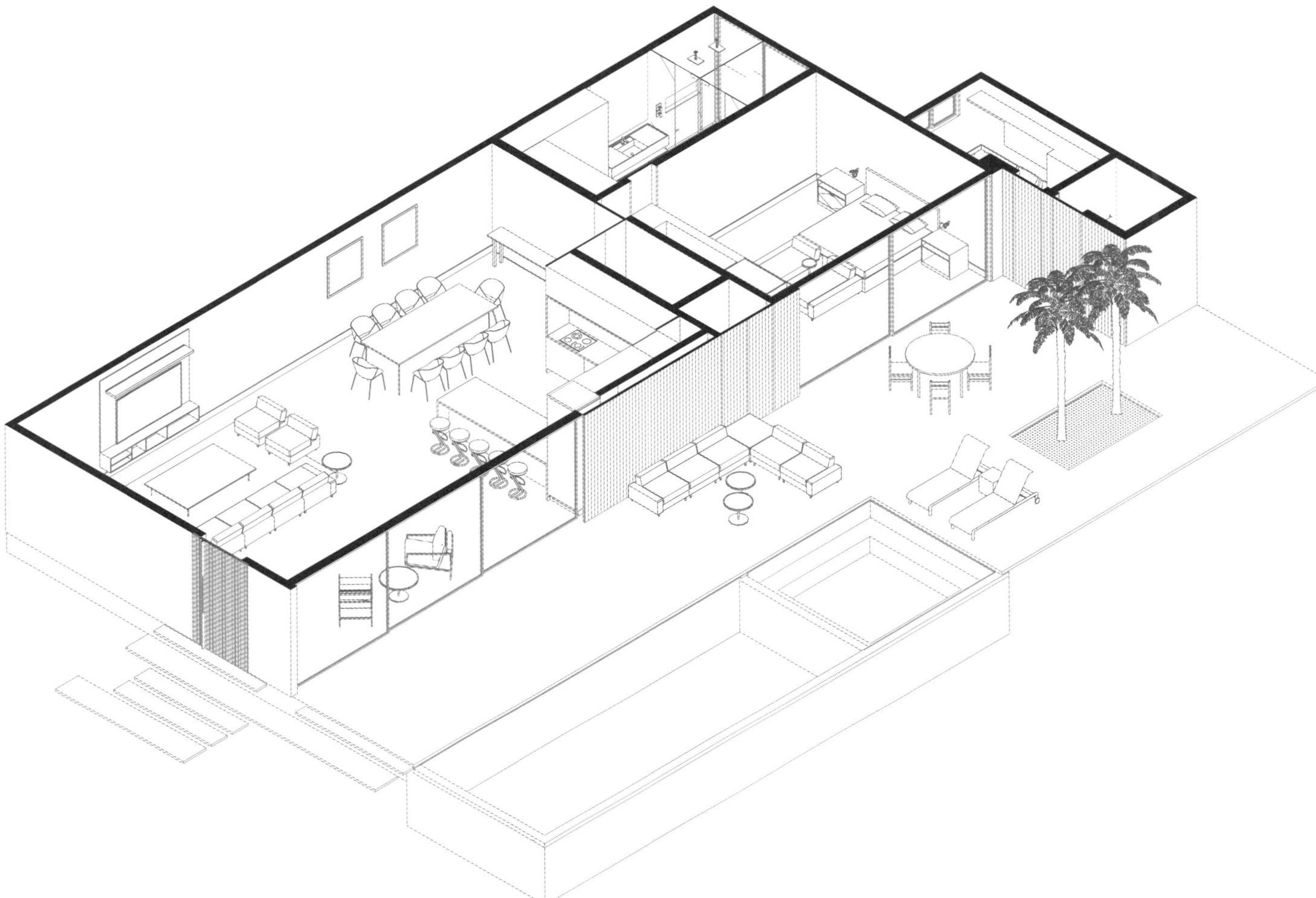

I

H View of the main façade overlooking the garden
I Axonometry

WAYANAD HOUSE

A

93

OTHER CREATIVES
Sandeep Khosla and Amaresh Anand
YEAR
2020
AREA
1,840 m²
NUMBER OF ROOMS
12
FURTHER FACTS
Central Skylit courtyard, balconies and verandahs as usable transition spaces in a heavy rainfall area
PHOTOGRAPHY
Shamanth Patil J.

Wayanad House is situated in a clearing in the midst of 60 hectares of dense coffee plantation. A large skylight-covered courtyard allows the natural light and lush tropical vegetation to flow into the interior. Surrounding verandas on the lower level and balconies on the upper floor connect the indoor and outside worlds. The ground floor largely consists of public areas, enveloping a veranda at the entrance and affording a view of the cascading water feature, as well as further inner courtyards and verandas. The master bedroom and guest rooms are situated there for the large family. The sizeable sliding doors and windows were strategically placed to enable cross-ventilation in the humid environment. The upper level accommodates private rooms for the inner family. An earthy color palette characterizes the building's materials: Yellow Jaiselmer stone, wood, gray kota stone, polished cement, and the local red laterite complement the green surroundings. The landscape design played a key role in establishing a gentle connection between the house and the existing forest countryside. Robust, local plants were used, while the flow of rainwater through the terrain was preserved.

A North elevation of Wayanad House at dusk
B View of the entrance

B

C

D

C View of the glass covered central courtyard
D Wood-paneled loggia with panoramic view
E Exterior view from the garden at night

E

F Interior view of the informal dining area
G The bright living room with skylight

F

G

H I

H Ground floor plan
I First floor plan

MEKONG HOUSE

YEAR
2021
AREA
200 m^2
NUMBER OF ROOMS
4
PHOTOGRAPHY
Spaceshift Studio

Mekong House expresses the owner's grounded character, the Mekong River environment, and the simple, locally typical architecture. The horizontal line of the façade mirrors the line of the river. All architectural elements have a simple, modest design. The open floor plan enables natural ventilation and affords a wonderful view of the river. Wooden balconies on the second floor act as shady, transitory spaces. Auxiliary functions such as bathrooms are accommodated in a concrete core to allow the other areas to enjoy maximum openness toward the natural surroundings. The main material is reused wood from a rice mill. The hand-crafted tectonics nestle into the countryside and conform to the owner's idea of being part of nature. The materials, including wooden shingles and beams, change with the climate. The project creates a modest and yet luxurious residence that is closely connected to nature, all implemented with a north-eastern, vernacular architecture that harmonizes with the Mekong River.

A Extorior view of Mekong House
B Dining and living area open to the garden

B

101

C Aerial view of the house overlooking the Mekong River

C

D

E F

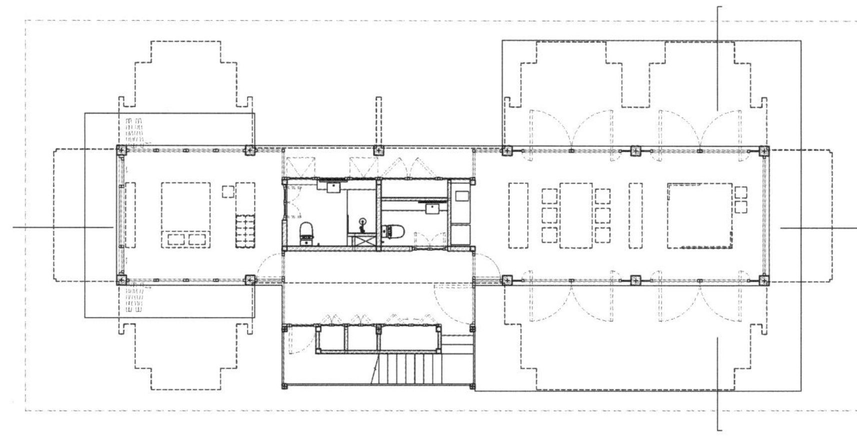

G

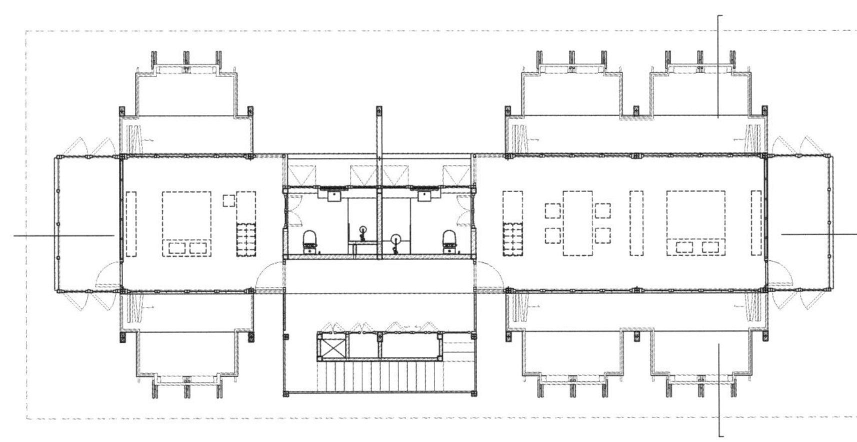

H

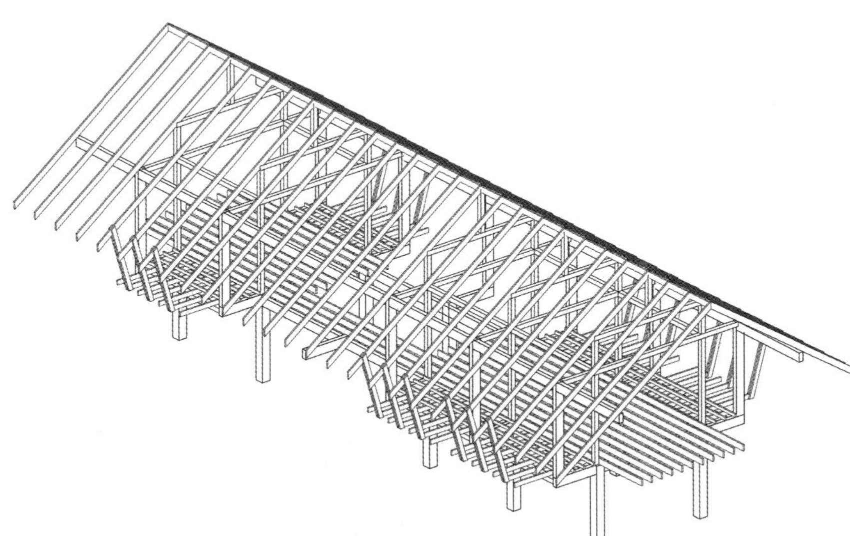

I

D Main view of the house from the garden
E Exterior wood stairs
F Covered balconies overlooking the beach
G First floor plan
H Second floor plan
I Isonometric structure

THE GRITTED GRID

A

YEAR
2021
AREA
1,450 m^2
NUMBER OF ROOMS
16
PHOTOGRAPHY
Mario Wibowo Photography

Although this building must fulfill many different demands and functions, instead of falling apart into its individual components, it remains calm and holistic through the specially designed honey-colored façade, uniting all of its zones. The varying façade composition achieves an artful interplay between transparency and seclusion, as well as outward and inward views. Three façades were enveloped by tailored fiber-cement breeze blocks, acting like a second skin, while remaining permeable to allow the light and the surroundings through. The relationship to the natural environment plays a major role in the design. It seems to flow through the house, filling the rooms with an exquisite atmosphere. The result is a beautiful balance between opulence, individual charm, and nature.

A Exterior view of Gritted Grid
B View from the master balcony separating the private space from the outside environment

B

C

C The floating staircase above a Koi pond
D View from the pool through the outdoor decking patio to the indoor living area
E Interior view of the double-height living room

D

LOEWE

F

G

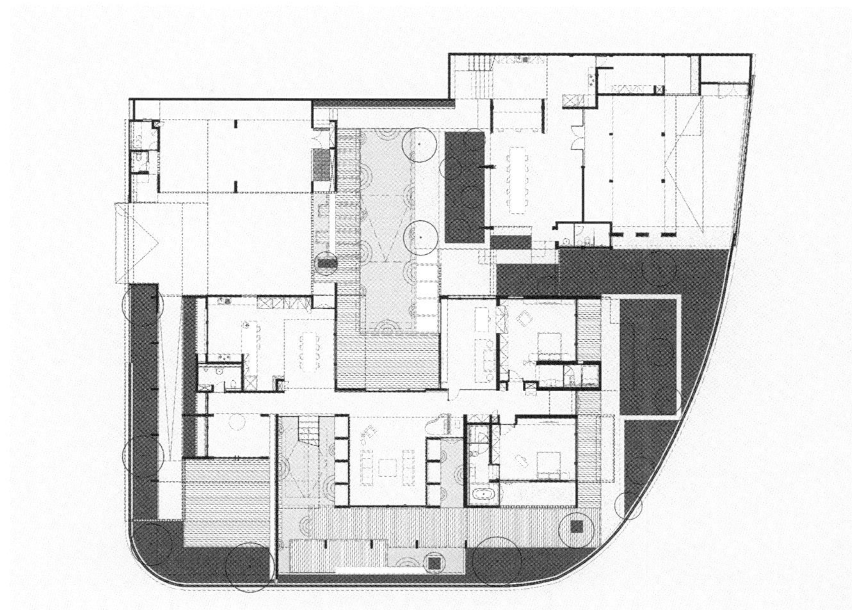

H

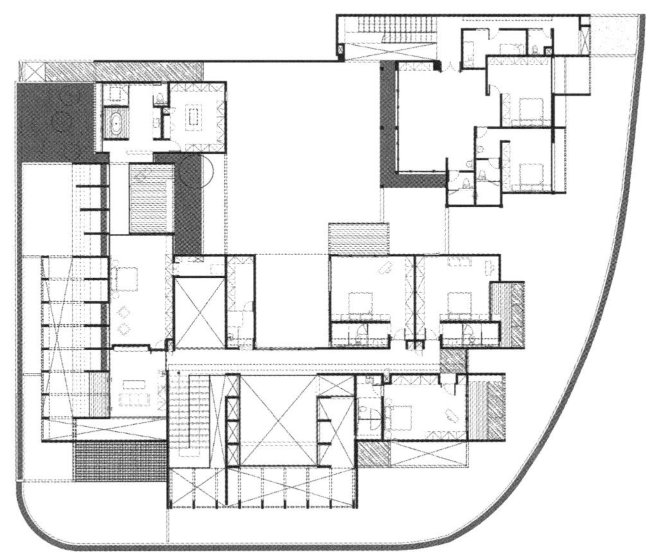

I

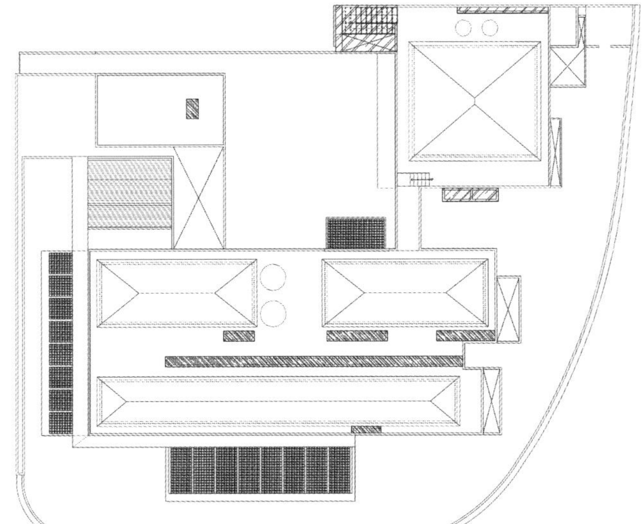

J

F View of the exterior façade wrapped with honey-colored custom fiber-cement breeze block
G Interior view of the master bedroom
H First floor plan
I Second floor plan
J Roof plan

THE ALIA

YEAR
2022
AREA
2,500 m^2
NUMBER OF ROOMS
18
PHOTOGRAPHY
Indra Wira, Bali

The Alia is a private family residence in Bali, consisting of two parts: the main building and the private club house. The development is situated in southern Bali, near Sunset Road. In a first construction stage, the house was built on a plot with a size of 2,500 square meters. The modern, tropical design includes wood, stone, and tile elements. The entrance mainly uses semi-transparent materials to create a private atmosphere, while allowing natural light to enter the foyer. The rooms are divided into three areas: the service area, private spaces, and a connection to the public zone. The living space and the pool were placed at the center of the plot, acting as the main, public area and visually connecting the individual zones. The bedrooms are mainly situated on the upper level. The communal spaces are grouped around the central pool, acting as its frame.

A View of house Alia from the terrace
B The living room with a spiral staircase

B

C Night view of the house from the garden

C

D E

F

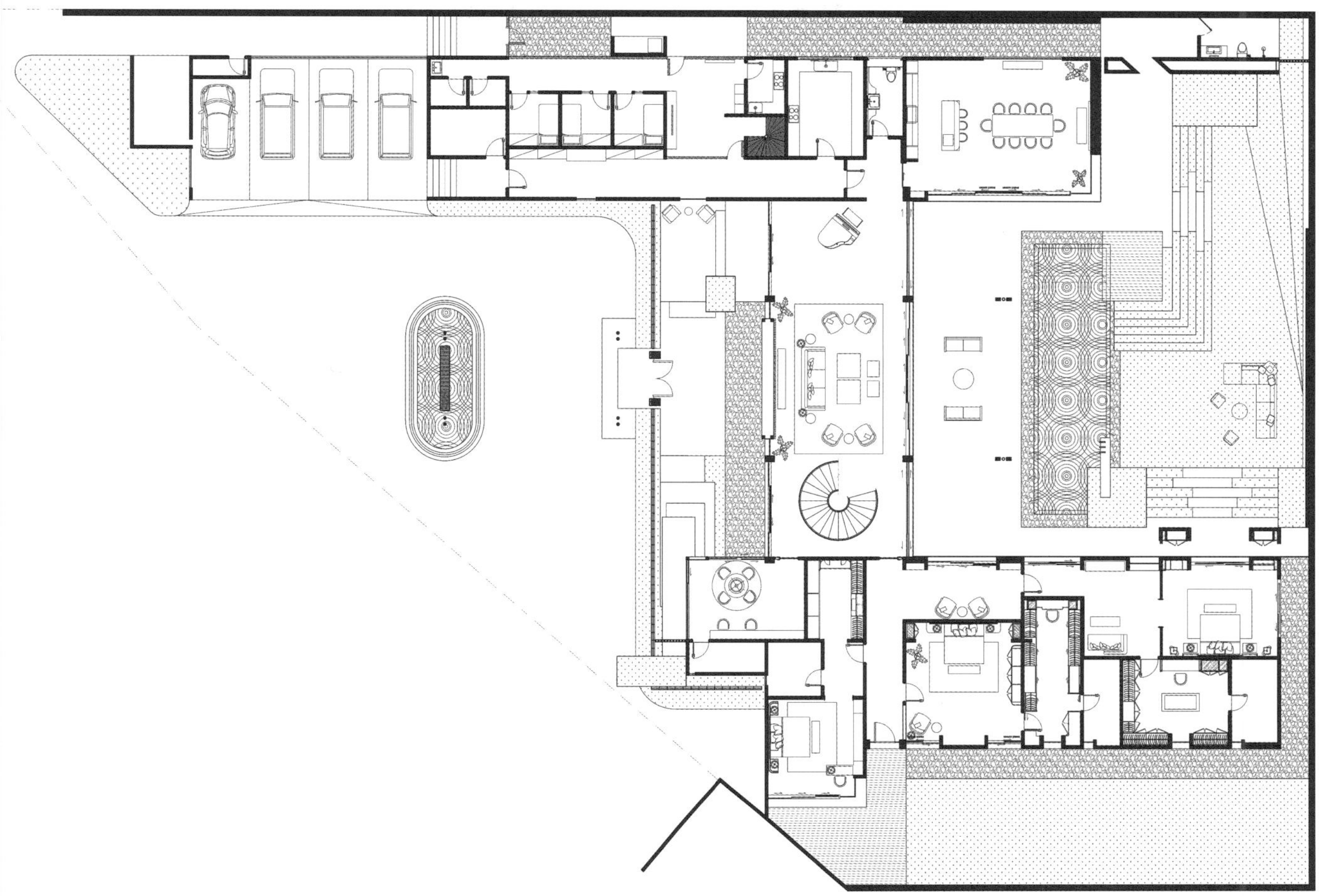

G

D View of the main entrance
E Side view of the pool and covered terrace
F Living room open to the terrace
G First floor plan

HOUSE OF SCREENS

A

OTHER CREATIVES
Patrick Espiritu and Spencer Sy Principal Architects, Neil Sandico Team Lead

YEAR
2022

AREA
700 m^2

NUMBER OF ROOMS
4

FURTHER FACTS
Pocket garden and screen louvers

PHOTOGRAPHY
Greg Mayo

The House of Screens artfully blends beauty, craftsmanship, and functionality. The three-story, 700 square meters building is situated on a sloping terrain and consists of two interlocking volumes. Its many window and door apertures can be closed using teak screens, thereby shielding the household from the heat and prying eyes. Sharp-edged eaves provide shade and highlight the building's horizontality, which is broken up by lush greenery. A dark stone-clad corridor leads to a bright, double-height space. The house's interior is characterized by natural colors and materials that exude abundant warmth. Private rooms such as the bedrooms and family room are elevated, affording beautiful views of the green surroundings. The ground-floor living and dining zone opens up toward a peaceful pool. An underground cave was excavated into the hillside, offering a secluded retreat.

A Front façade of House of Screens
B Open living area overlooking the patio, with bespoke furniture

B

C

D

E F

C Night view of the pool and covered terrace
D Open dining and kitchen area
E View of the façades facing the interior patio
F Detail of the lush flora at the main entrance

G H

I

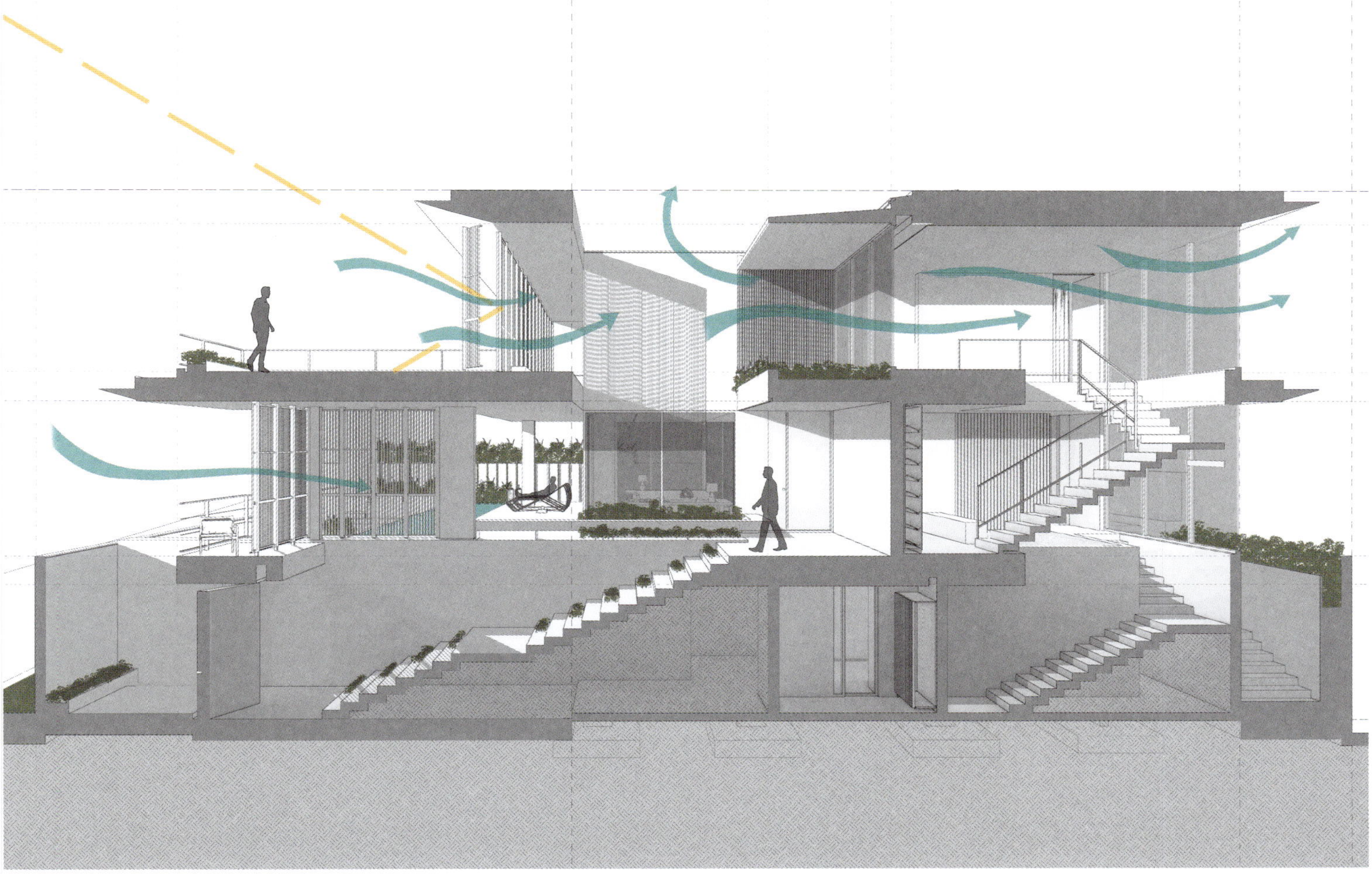

J

G Master bathroom
H Interior view of the master bedroom
I View of the screened façade at dusk
J Longitudinal section

VILLAS 72

A

123

OTHER CREATIVES
Grupo Wawa
YEAR
2022
AREA
818 m²
NUMBER OF ROOMS
9
FURTHER FACTS
Three houses
PHOTOGRAPHY
Alejandra Urquiza, Alonso Velarde and Daniel Macias

The interplay of light, reflections, and local materials highlight the concept's monochrome spaces. The textures of wood, limestone, and exposed keystone enable an economic, sustainable, and bioclimatic design, offering a wealth of qualities in the atmospheric rooms. The villas consist of two key elements: a high gallery serving as a communicative space, and a second volume with three rooms and a parking space. The rooms' optimized arrangement offers shady terraces and usable outdoor spaces. Originally designed as a permanent residence, the project developed into rented villas for various users. A combination of refined elements of locally typical architecture connects the development to the center of Mérida. The elegance and simplicity of the Villas 72 have created a unique, peaceful place in the historical center of Mérida that is harmoniously integrated into the surrounding landscape.

A Main view of the entrances of Villas 72
B Detail of the interior stairs with vegetation

B

C D

E

C Interior view of the dining and kitchen area
D The terrace from above
E View of the façade overlooking the interior terrace with large windows
F View of the double-height living room

F

G

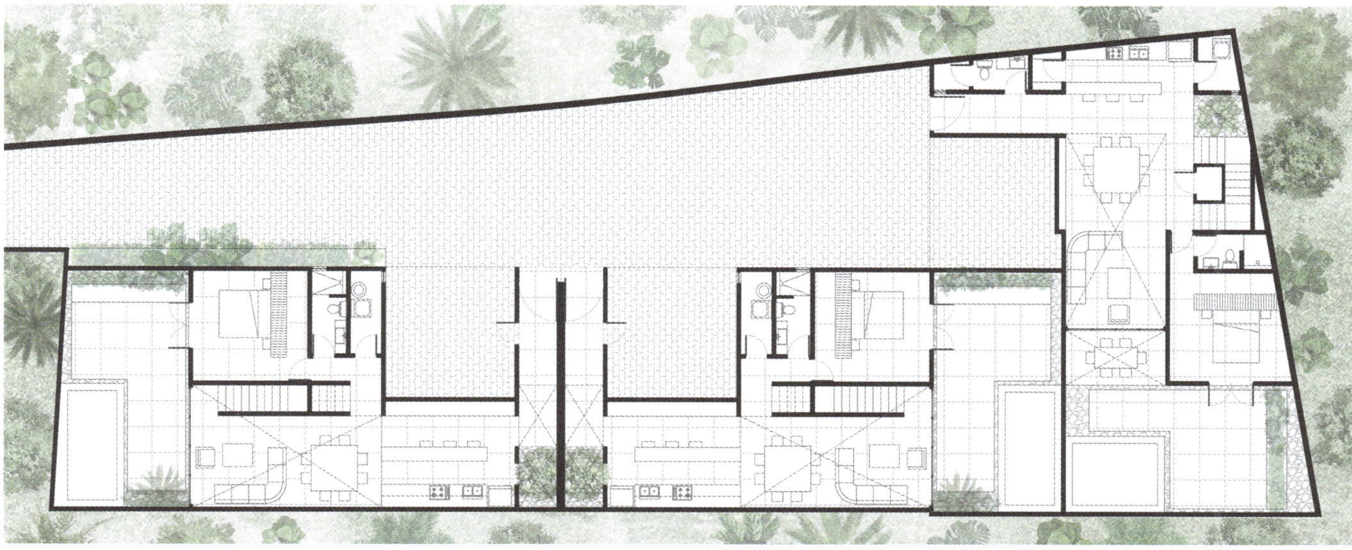

H

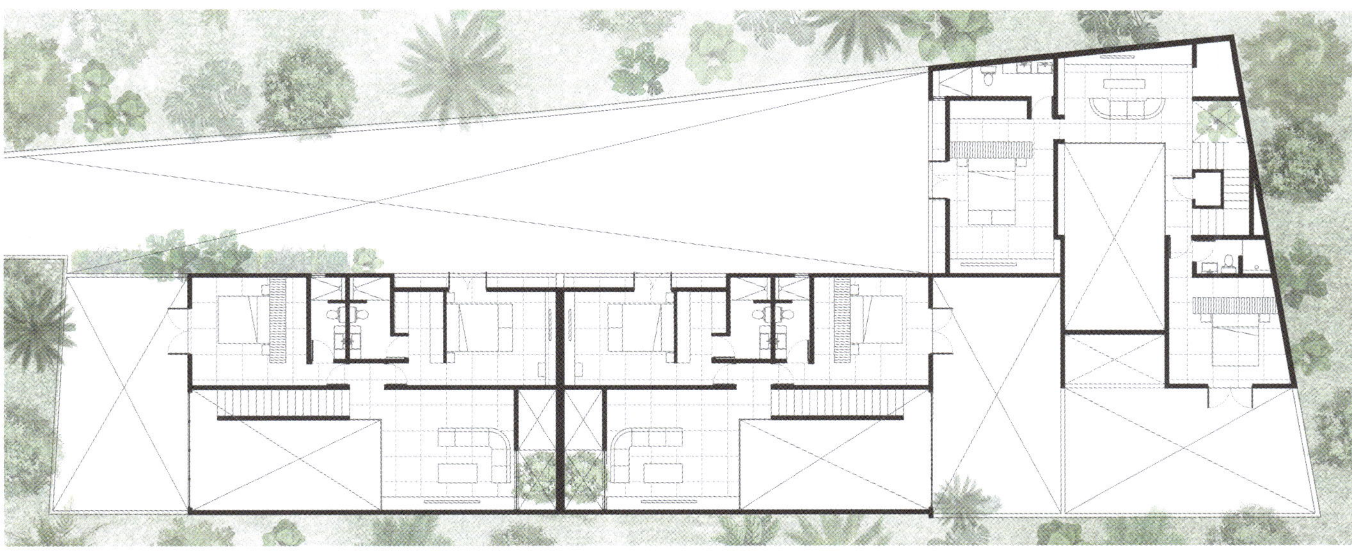

I

G View of the terrace with pool and cozy corner with hammock
H First floor plan
I Second floor plan

HOUSE OF TONINHAS

A

OTHER CREATIVES
Gustavo Tenca and Inácio Cardona
YEAR
2020
AREA
512 m²
NUMBER OF ROOMS
7
PHOTOGRAPHY
Adriano Pacelli

The summer residence in Ubatuba, 230 kilometers away from São Paulo, is situated on a steep slope in the midst of a dense Atlantic forest. Nature and the topography are the design's key inspirations. The entrance was designed to overcome the terrain in a straight line, framing the view of the sea and attracting attention to the rooftop terrace, which offers a spectacular view. The clearly structured floor plan sensibly zones the different use areas and aligns them toward the sea and the forest. The materials were chosen and combined with care, especially the metallic Cobogó on the façade and the dominant natural materials such as granilite, wood, and aluminum slats, which create an exciting interplay of transparency and seclusion. Slatted panels and sliding glass elements control and guide the sunlight exposure, while abundant natural light and cross-ventilation ensure comfortable temperatures.

A View of the main entrance of House of Toninhas
B External staircase overlooking the sea

B

C Main view of House of Toninhas surrounded by nature

C

D E

F

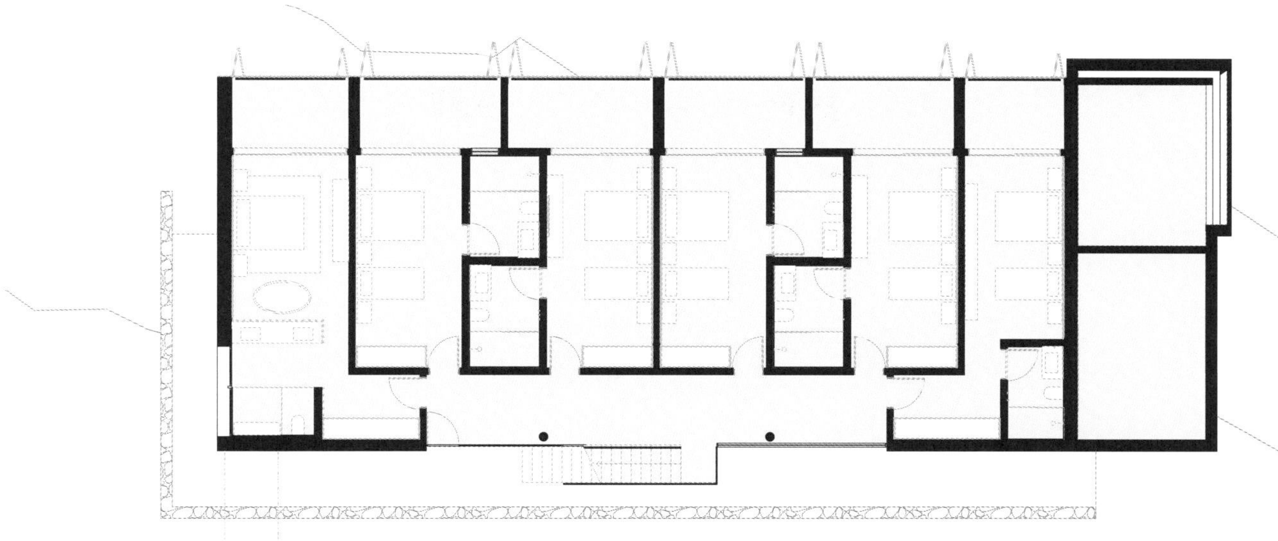

G

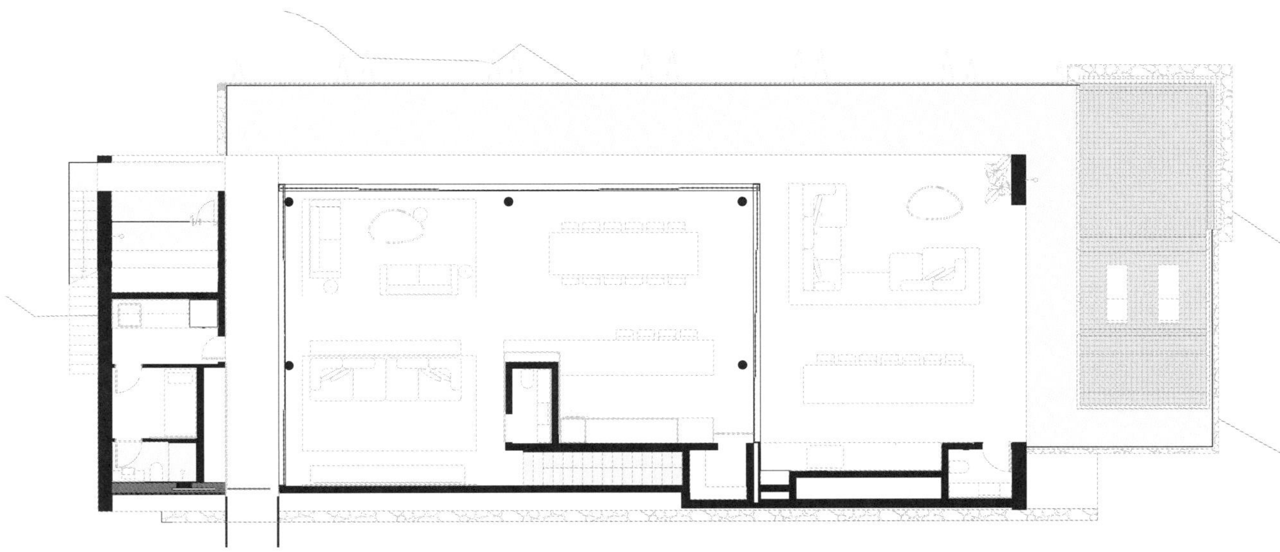

H

D View from the beach of the house surrounded by nature
E Living area with ocean view
F House view from the pool
G Lower floor plan
H First floor plan

134

FBW URBANISTS + ARCHITECTS

HOUSE MBWENI

A

YEAR
2019
AREA
296 m²
NUMBER OF ROOMS
8
PHOTOGRAPHY
Alexandra Papadaki, Franka van Marrewijk

House Mbweni sets itself apart from the copy-paste housing of the surrounding upmarket residential neighborhood by evoking austerity in a modest, but distinct volume. The project's autonomous and locally typical building method reacts to its specific climatic and cultural surroundings. The house was designed as a box in a box and is situated diagonally on a platform to ensure a long vista. The concept uses double façades and an inverted roof over a flat roof. The verandas, loggias, balconies, and galleries, which form part of the double façade, create an intermediate world between the garden and the interior. This buffer zone achieves an interplay between private and public spaces, while also ensuring shading for subdued, attractive light conditions. The inverted roof collects rainwater for use in the house, while a park of rooftop solar collectors provides power and hot water.

A East façade of House Mbweni
B Entrance hall illuminated by morning light

B

C View of the veranda
D Interior view of the living area with a large window overlooking the pool
E Exterior façade with screened walls

C

D

E

F

G

F House view from the pool
G Interior view of the corridor with morning light
H First floor plan
I Second floor plan

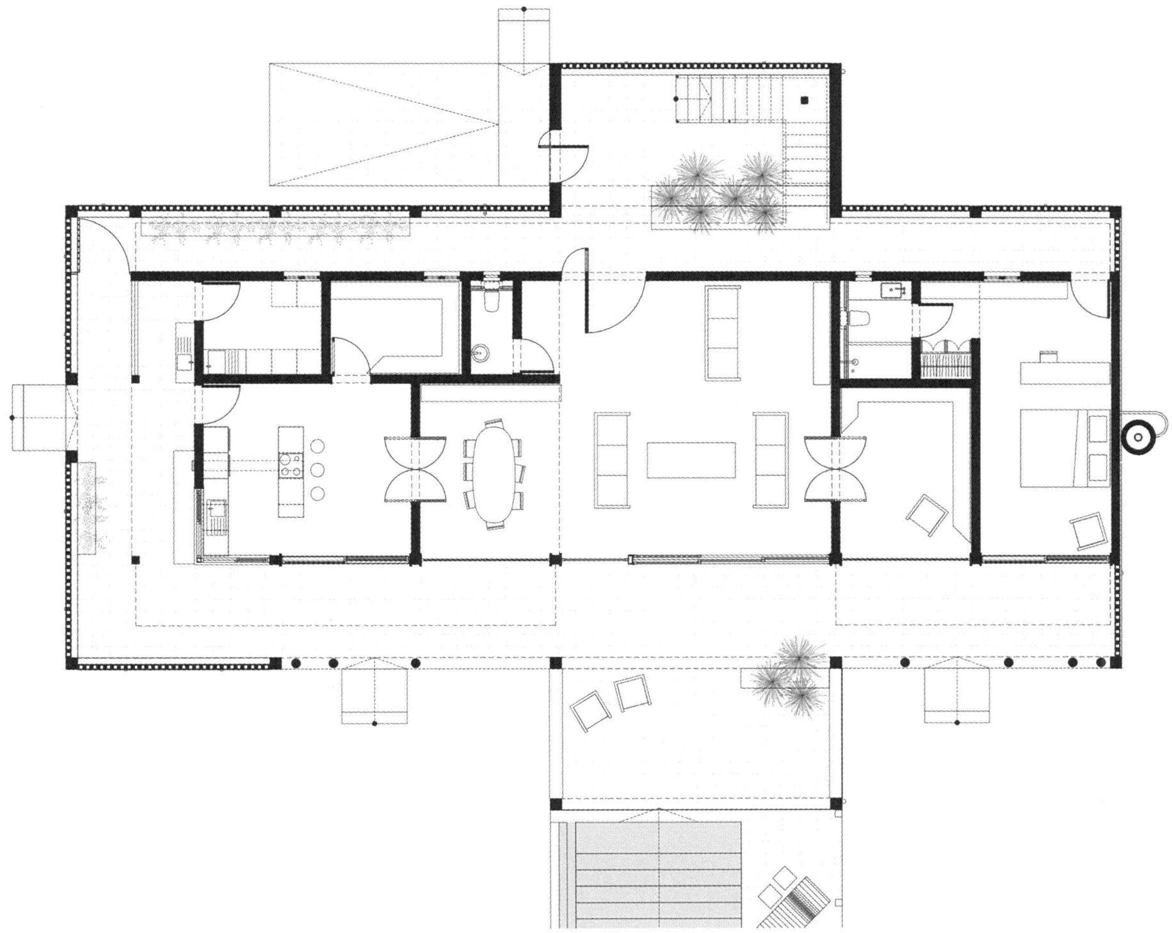

H

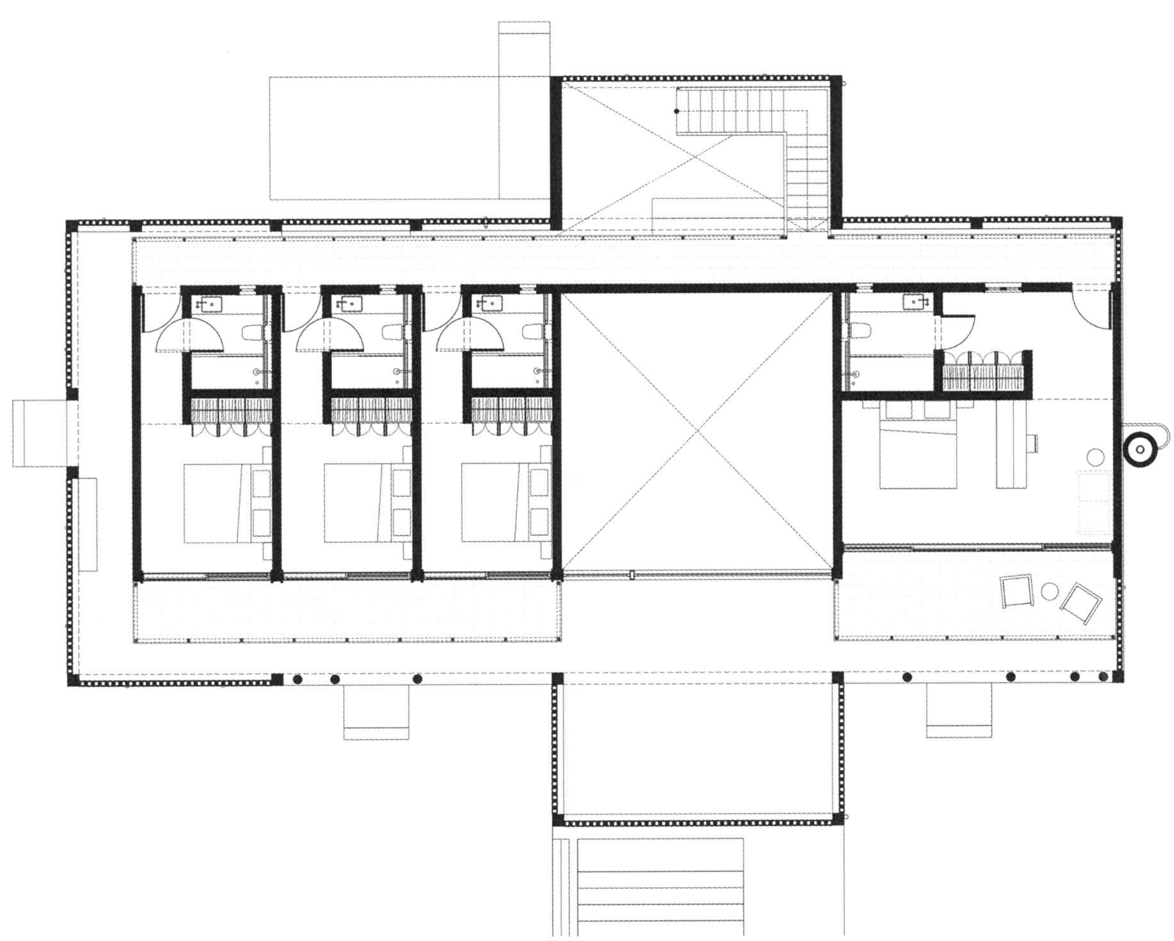

I

OHIO HOUSE

YEAR
2022
AREA
505.7 m^2
NUMBER OF ROOMS
17
FURTHER FACTS
Breathing perforated metal stairs, rotating vertical fins as secondary skin
PHOTOGRAPHY
studioRK, Jakarta

StudioRK's OHIO House design was primarily inspired by the way nature constantly creates fascinating spaces. The exterior areas, terraces, balconies, and entrances are defined by the shade that the lining trees provide, filtering the sunlight and wind through their swaying leaves. This green perimeter, forming a buffer between the exterior grounds and private areas, acts as a living privacy shield, while allowing sufficient light and air to enter the building. The transition between interior and exterior spaces remains fluent, allowing the zones to be used flexibly. OHIO House responds to global resource problems with intelligent energy-saving solutions. These include green areas on the ground and façade, as well as passive cooling systems, optimized natural lighting, and windows that can be opened wide, with breathable insect netting. The playful approach to the volume creates a wealth of open spaces for nature and the users themselves.

A Front view of OHIO House
B Outdoor seating surrounded by trees and koi pond

B

C Breathing perforated staircase
D Living Room intimately connected to surroundings
E View from living room overlooking outdoor seating surrounded by trees
F Children's bedroom

C

D

E

F

G

H

I

G Rooftop garden with 270 degrees skyline view
H View of the pool with tropical jungle in the backyard
I Preliminary sketch showing the connection between spaces and nature

ANGEL OAKS

OTHER CREATIVES
La Casona Garden Landscape
YEAR
2021
AREA
930 m²
NUMBER OF ROOMS
12
PHOTOGRAPHY
Kris Tamburello, Miami

Angel Oaks is an architectural masterpiece situated on an oversized plot on the outskirts of Miami. The building is organized around a central courtyard that opens up toward the landscape and accommodates a linear pool and terrace. Two distinctive wings are connected by a two-story bridge above the main living room. Large walls made of split-face keystone welcome visitors and create a smooth transition between interior and exterior zones. The "outdoor living room" around the pool offers a daring span, while the second floor with its wooden shutters offers privacy for the bedrooms and family room. The minimalist, modern design complements the elegant landscaping and surrounding garden.

A Exterior view of Angel Oaks House from the pool terrace
B View of the living area completely open to the garden

B

C Main view of the house from the front entrance garden

C

D E

F

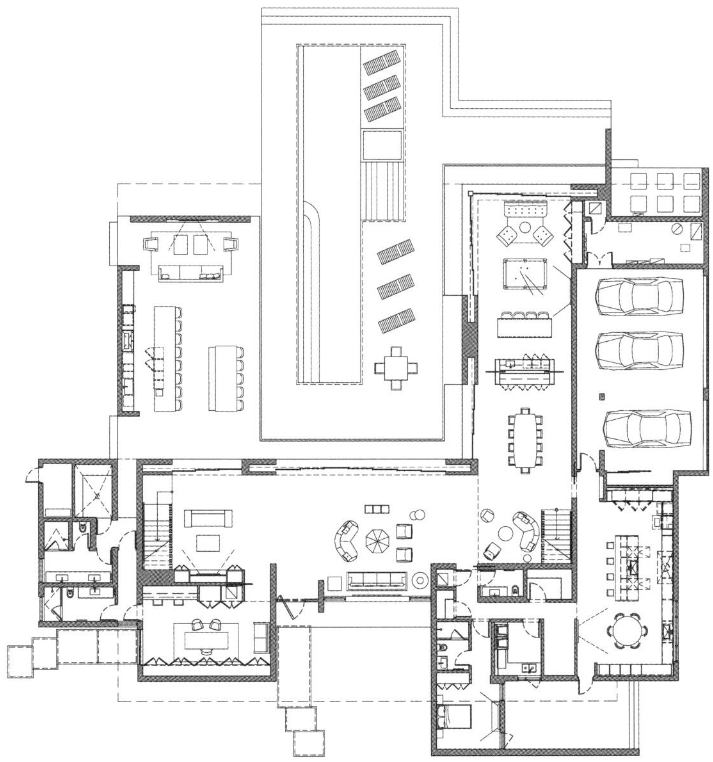

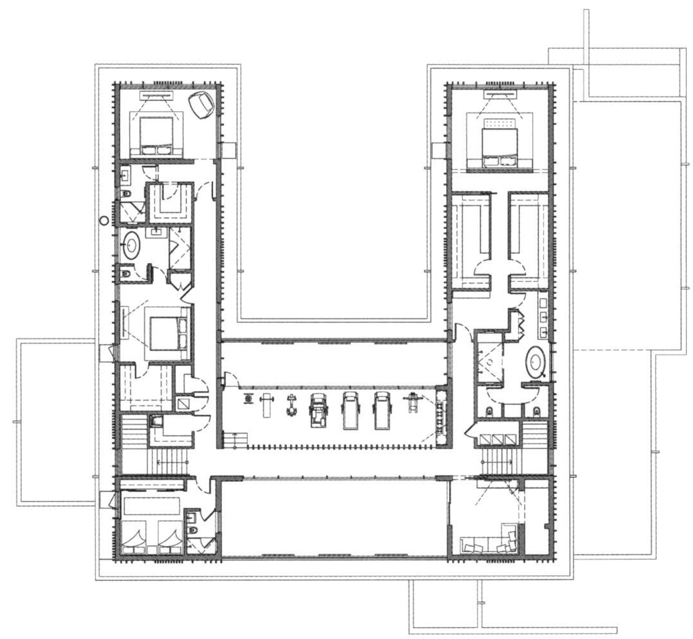

G H

D View of the dining room with windows overlooking the terrace
E Interior view of the master bedroom
F Exterior view of the sauna from the wooden terrace with pool
G First floor plan
H Second floor plan

HIDDEN GARDEN HOUSE

A

153

YEAR
2023
AREA
1,500 m²
NUMBER OF ROOMS
6
PHOTOGRAPHY
William Susanto

The house in the Menteng region, a renowned, historical neighborhood, is an innovative response to the existing glamorous Menteng buildings. With a size of 1,500 m², it represents an urban tropical experiment that reconsiders scale and space. The ground floor is open and transparent, without partition walls, thereby allowing visual relationships, as well as housing a pool as a light-reflection line, and a skylight for the basement. The house follows a very special approach in combining several gardens and neighborhoods in a single building. The rooftop landscape is connected to the surrounding urban landscape, while multistory gardens provide open, elegant inward views. The architecture strives not only to achieve beauty, by also focuses on energy efficiency, using passive and active building elements. The seamless connection between interior and exterior spaces produces an inviting atmosphere and an elegant, contemporary design. The home is the result of a young family's search to fulfill the requirements of its unique lifestyle.

A Main view of the indoor patio of Hidden Garden House
B Exterior view of the roof garden
C View of the tropical garden on the mezanine floor

B C

D Sky rooftop with a view of Jakarta city
E Mezanine floor surrounded by plants
F Multiple views inside different rooms of the house

D

E

F

G

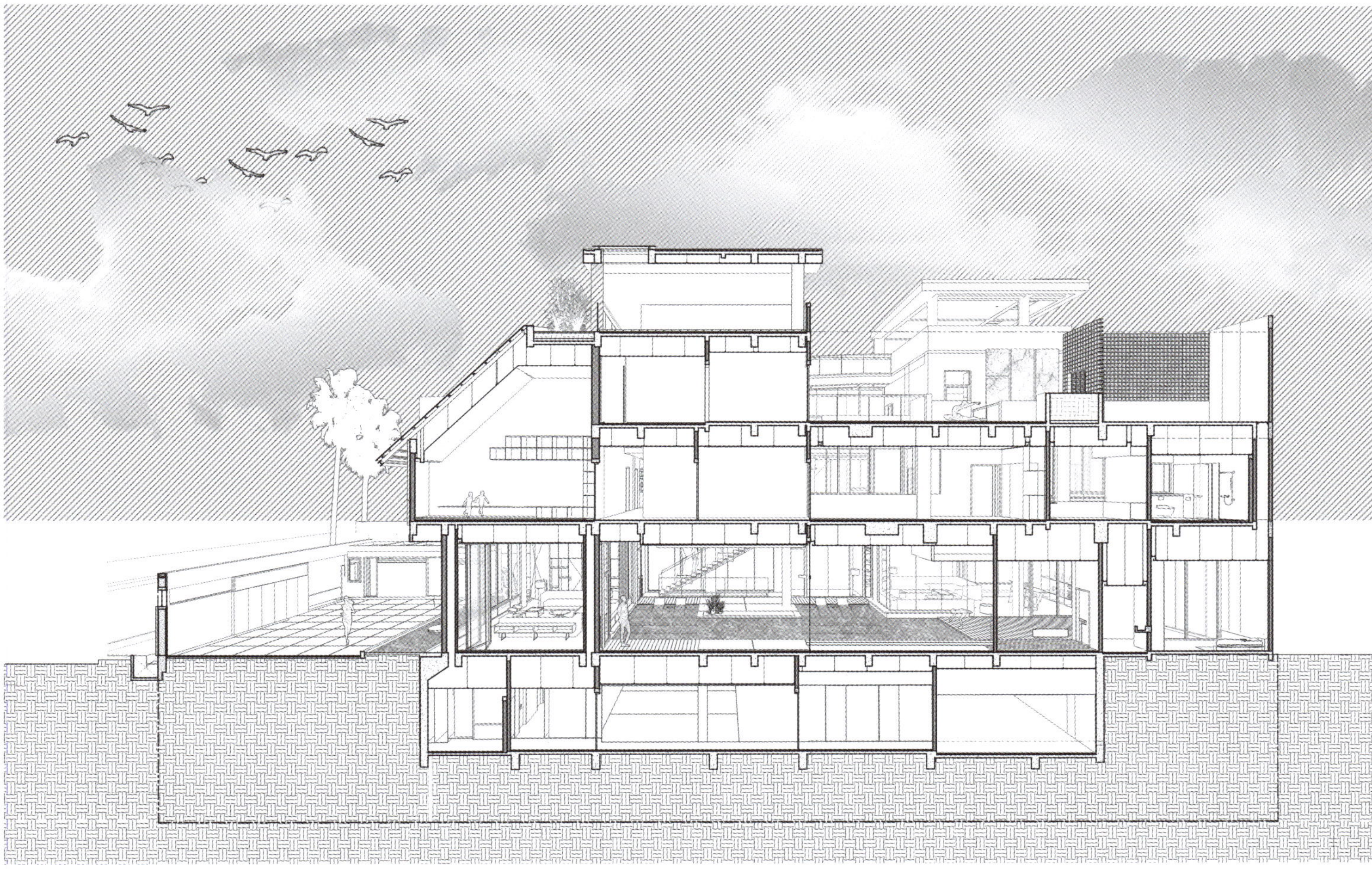

H

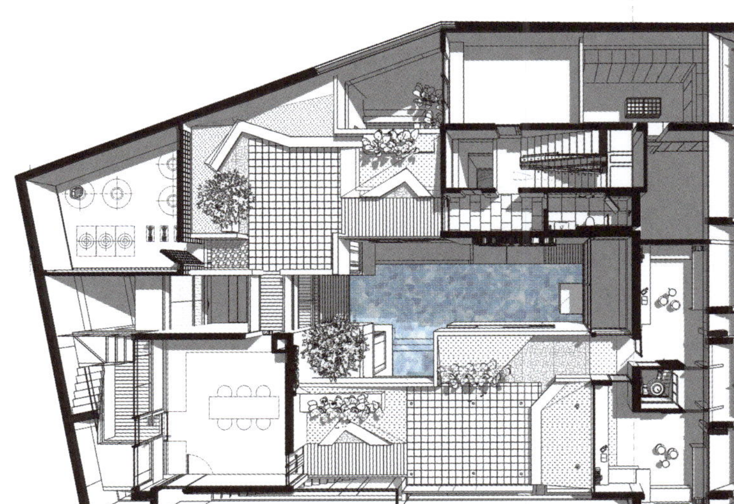

I

G View of the different volumes of the house overlooking the indoor pool
H Longitudinal section of Hidden Garden House
I Mezanine floor plan

FIREFLY HOUSE

A

YEAR
2021
AREA
350 m²
NUMBER OF ROOMS
7
FURTHER FACTS
Traditional Thai space in modern style house, Coconut concrete formwork
PHOTOGRAPHY
Volume Matrix Studio, Bangkok

The house designed for the owner's mother represents a family space for different generations to live together. Following an on-site meeting, the architects learned that the plot was a coconut garden that had deep-rooted memories for the family. The design is based on the idea of integrating that garden, which the grandmother had tended to. The architecture was divided into small, contrasting volumes depending on their function, allowing them to fit in the garden. The volumes' different heights create terraces between the rooms and the "Tai Thun", a space beneath Thai houses that allows the breeze to pass through all rooms. To preserve the original atmosphere, local materials were reused, including old wood for the inner walls and metal panels as a sun-shield. The bedroom's metal façade has many perforations, thereby resembling a lace curtain. During the day, it provides protection from the sun, while still allowing the garden silhouette to be visible through the holes. The design combines family memories, traditional elements, and modern aesthetics.

A Firefly House behind the coconut grove
B Interior view of the dining area open to the garden

B

C

D

E

F

C Details of the exterior façade.
D View of the kitchen area from the outside
E Interior view of one bedroom
F Firefly House at night from the garden

G

G View of the foyer
H Main view of the house from the garden

H

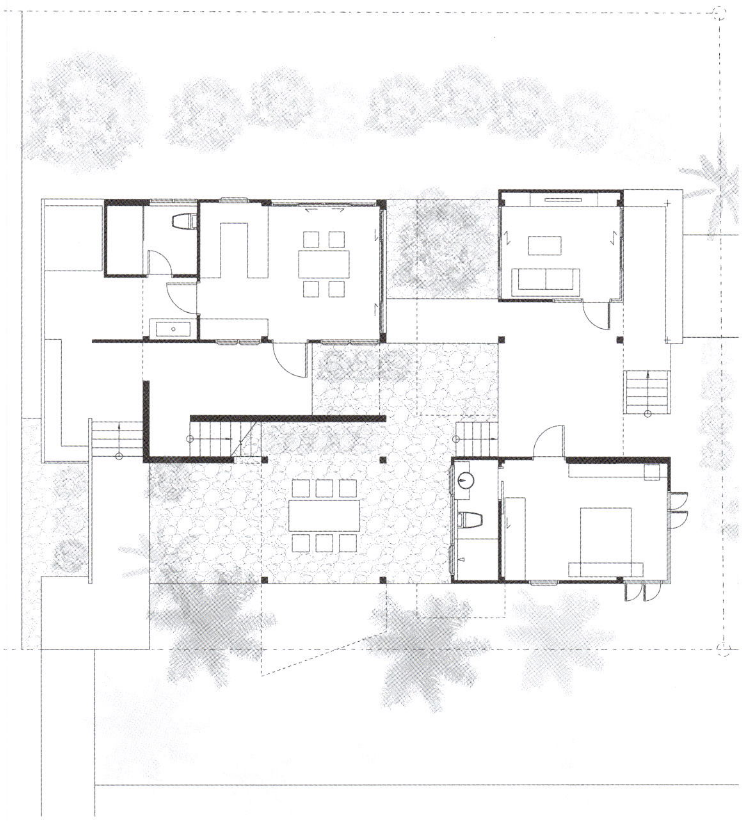

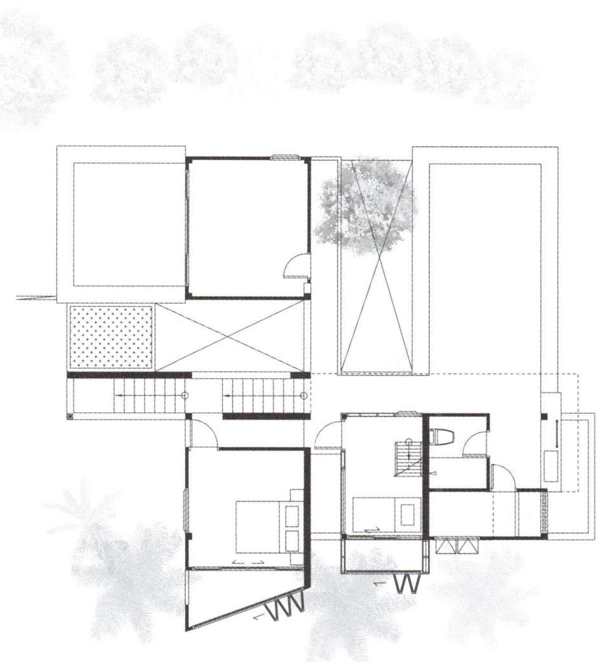

I J

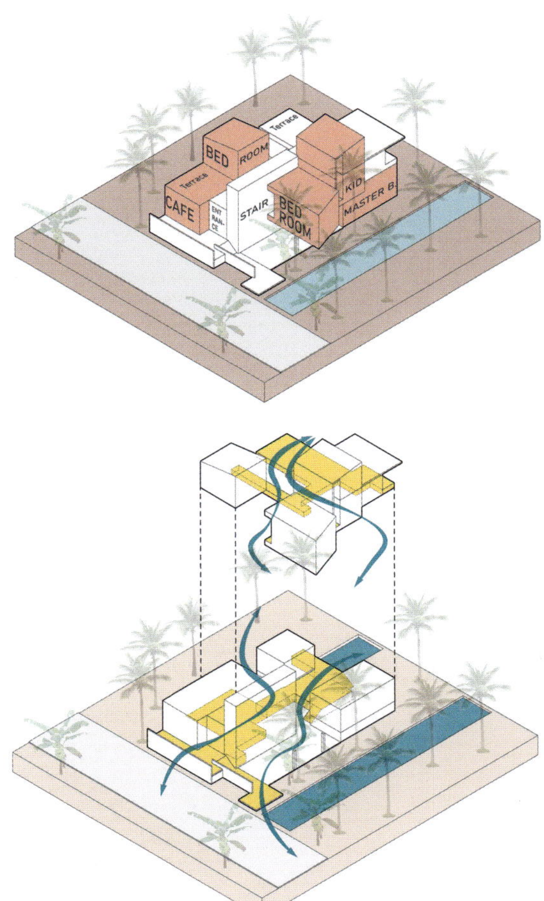

K

I First floor plan
J Second floor plan
K Design concept of Firefly House

CONCHAS HOUSE

A

OTHER CREATIVES
Arquitetura Gui Mattos Interior Design
YEAR
2015
AREA
807 m²
NUMBER OF ROOMS
9
PHOTOGRAPHY
Leonardo Finotti, São Paulo

Conchas House is the only residence on the small beach along the north coast of São Paulo. It forms part of a small plateau, turns its back to the sloping terrain and the dense mountain forest, and embraces the sandy Praia das Conchas beach like an amphitheater. The building was inspired by the terrain's different elevations, entering into a dialogue with the landscape and ensuring that it is not lost in scale. Connected by a combination of contemporary and traditional languages, the two blocks are raised from the ground. The lower section accommodates the housekeeping bedrooms, the garage, and the service areas. The highest section of the topography surrounds a volume housing the six overlapping bedrooms. Placed linearly upon the descending terrain, a second volume provides social areas and follows the contours of the topography. It opens up strategically towards the gaps in the forest, offering a framed view of the islands on the horizon. The metal structure was conceived to allow an opening in the ridge, thereby minimizing differences between indoor and outdoor lighting conditions, as the changing natural light indicates the passage of time.

A Main entrance of Conchas House
B Side view of the open living area from the beach side

B

C D

E

F

G

C Panoramic view from the pool at twilight
D Exterior façade with wood cladding
E Outdoor terrace with infinity pool overlooking the beach
F View of the living area open to the surrounding landscape
G Detail of the wooden shutters in the bedrooms

H

I

H Open living area
I View of the corridor leading the stairs
J First floor plan
K Second floor plan

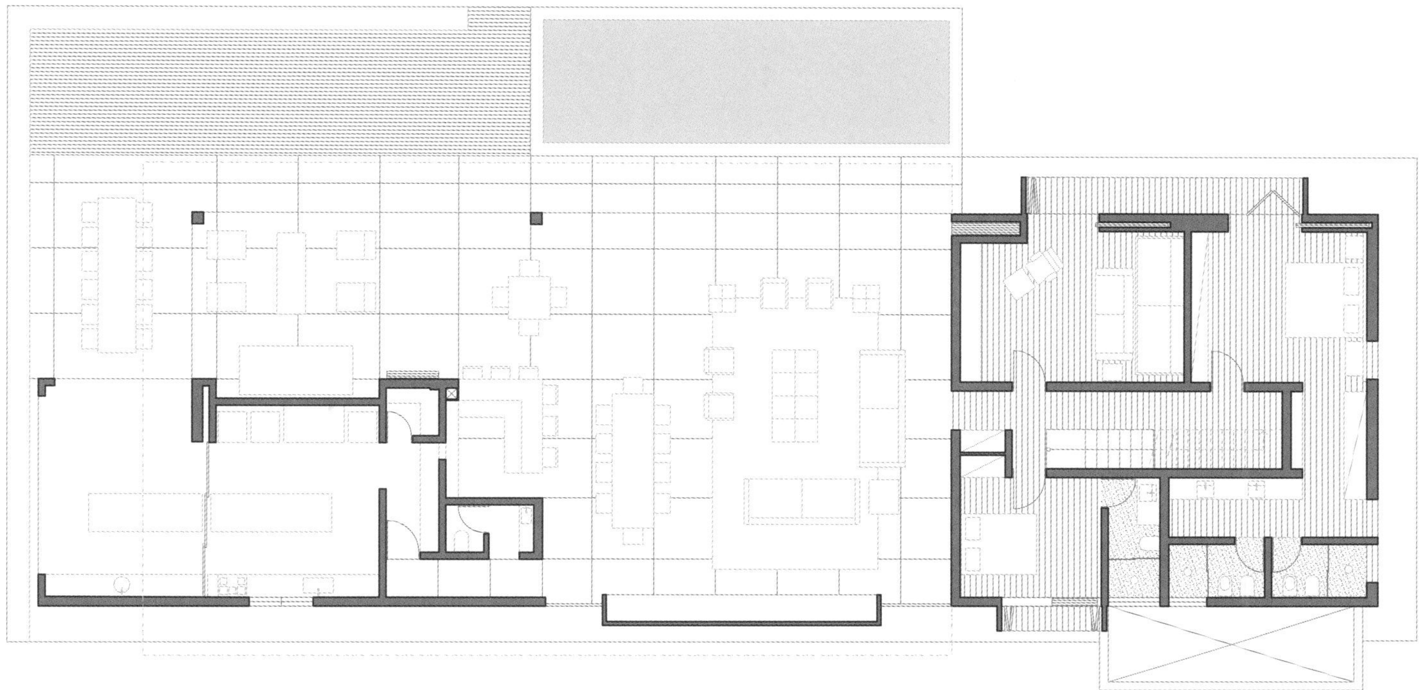

J

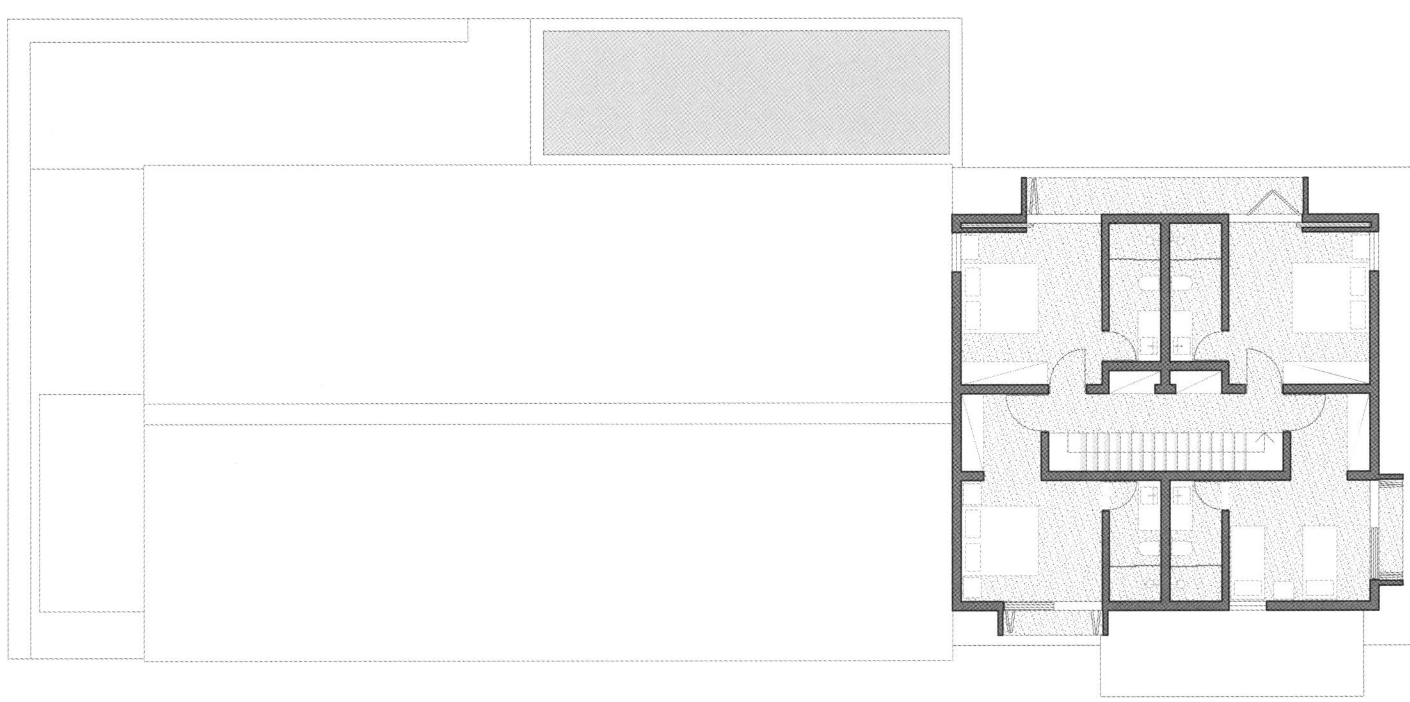

K

CORNER HOUSE

A

OTHER CREATIVES
Studiotripleone
YEAR
2022
AREA
1,200 m²
NUMBER OF ROOMS
10
FURTHER FACTS
An internal courtyard towards the corner of the property accentuating the visual expanse
PHOTOGRAPHY
Lightzone India

Located on a prominent corner within the neighbourhood, the design leverages the opportunities of its multiple frontages making it experiential whilst engaging with the streetscape. This family residence is structured around a primary courtyard towards the side street, hence providing a larger visual open feel that connects to outdoor spaces with an expression sensitive to its surroundings. This courtyard essentially segregates the building into formal and informal areas intertwined via a staggered internal passage. To the front, formal space is scooped out to create a covered patio that in turn connects the front formal lawn with the internal court. The informal part of the house to the rear features an open plan kitchen, dining, and informal living with direct access to private garden spaces at the rear of the property. A wraparound timber louver system was developed as a screen for solar control, effectively forming a self-shading façade along the corner street.

A View of Corner House
B The upper level timber louvers extend into the courtyard

B

C Evening view of the house integrated into the landscape

C

D

E F

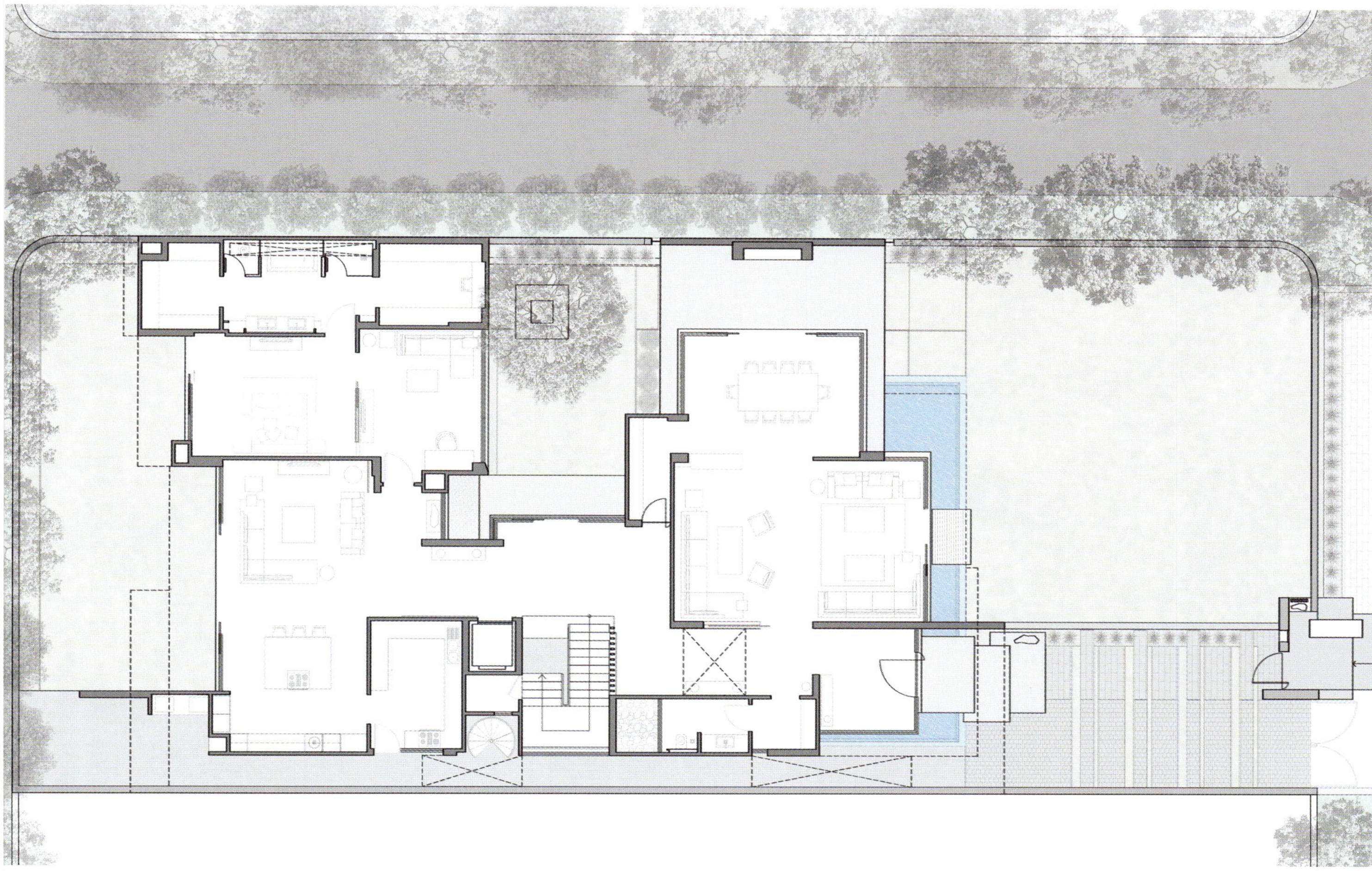

G

H

D View of the master lounge.
E Detail of the living room´s glazed extension floating over the reflective pool
F Interior view of the foyer
G Ground floor plan
H Section though courtyard

OUT OF THE BLUE

A

OTHER CREATIVES
HS2G landscape, Zvonimir T. Belfranin structural engineers, Energy Sciences MEP engineers, E. A. R. Management
YEAR
2018
AREA
464.5 m^2
NUMBER OF ROOMS
7
FURTHER FACTS
Bahamian inspired waterfront residence
PHOTOGRAPHY
Michael Stavaridis

This tropical house on the island of Cat Cay required a design that would ensure both a private atmosphere and a strong connection to the sea and the Bahamas. The design was inspired by the Bahamian culture and focuses on the challenges of coastal construction in times of climate change. The architecture comprises local window shutters, verandas, and materials such as limestone. The shady verandas ensure that the building remains cool and maintains a strong connection to the blue horizon. The outdoor grounds are as important as the interior, with overhanging concrete decks perched on the cliff, overlooking the beach below. The interior has an open, airy design, with large windows for natural lighting and broad sea views. The outdoor areas are designed to be inviting and functional, while entering into a respectful relationship with the surrounding environment.

A View of the dining and living area open to the terrace
B Exterior view of the house from the beach

B

C

D

E

F

C Exterior view of the entrance façade.
D Interior view of the bright living and kitchen area
E The outdoor living area on the pool terrace overlooking the ocean
F View of the main entrance

G

G Detail of the bathtub with ocean view
H Infinity pool from the cozy covered outdoor lounge

H

I

J

I Floor plan sketch
J Living area inspiration sketch

KALRAV

OTHER CREATIVES
PMC-SMI infrastructure
YEAR
2022
AREA
522.76 m^2
NUMBER OF ROOMS
3
FURTHER FACTS
The shape of the villa is inspired by a flying bird
PHOTOGRAPHY
Inclined Studio, Ahmedabad

This villa was designed as a tropical manifesto within the city. Inspired by a flying bird, it flaunts a wing-shaped roof with panoramic views from all sides within, designed with elegant materials: glass, exposed concrete, metal, and lime plaster. Maximum privacy is ensured in the dense green environment. Local materials and the landscape beneath – such as the green stairway to the open sky and elegant bath areas on the first floor – achieve a metaphorical tropicality. Elevated roofs ensure a magnificent view from the private rooms.

A View of Kalrav Villa surrounded by vegetation from above
B Interior view of the living area

B

C Façade view from the garden at twilight

C

D E

F

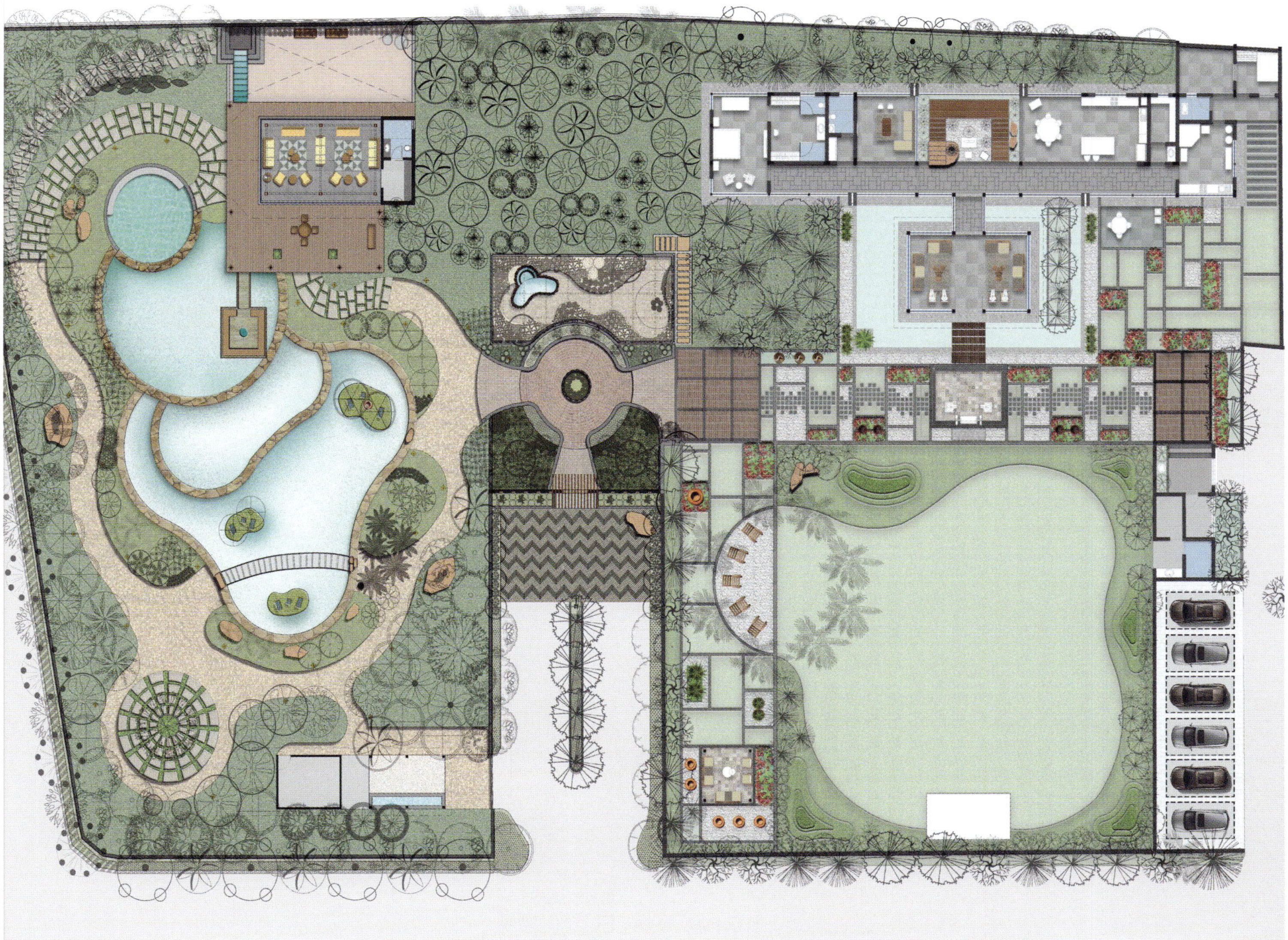

G

D Outdoor bath area on the first floor
E One bedroom with view of the surrounding nature
F Living area surrounded by the artificial pond
G Site plan

DS HOUSE

OTHER CREATIVES
Ady Putra Interior Designer, Artmosphere Lighting Consultant
YEAR
2022
AREA
460 m^2
NUMBER OF ROOMS
4
PHOTOGRAPHY
Ernest Theofilus

DS House impresses with its nature-based design and a strong connection to its surroundings. Embedded in lush greenery, its woven façade with complex patterns not only creates a dramatic atmosphere, but also serves as a filter offering targeted views of the garden. The interior design also focuses on nature and showcases specific perspectives. The open space on the second floor, its windows framing the garden landscape, allows natural light to enter the building, highlights the colors of the vegetation, and creates a pleasantly peaceful atmosphere. The adjoining multifunctional outdoor area, which is enveloped in woven materials, allows flexible usage in all weather conditions. The greenery continues up to the top level, the rooftop terrace. The oasis creates a quiet, introverted retreat, as interleaving interior and exterior spaces offer its residents an especially homely atmosphere.

A Main view of DS House with shuttered façade
B View of the foyer open to the nature of the patio

B

C D

E F

G

H

C Interior view of children's bedroom
D The master bedroom terrace
E View of a cozy outdoor seating area near the Koi pond
F Interior view of the hallway
G Dining and living area overlooking the outoor spaces
H Detail of the interior staircase

I

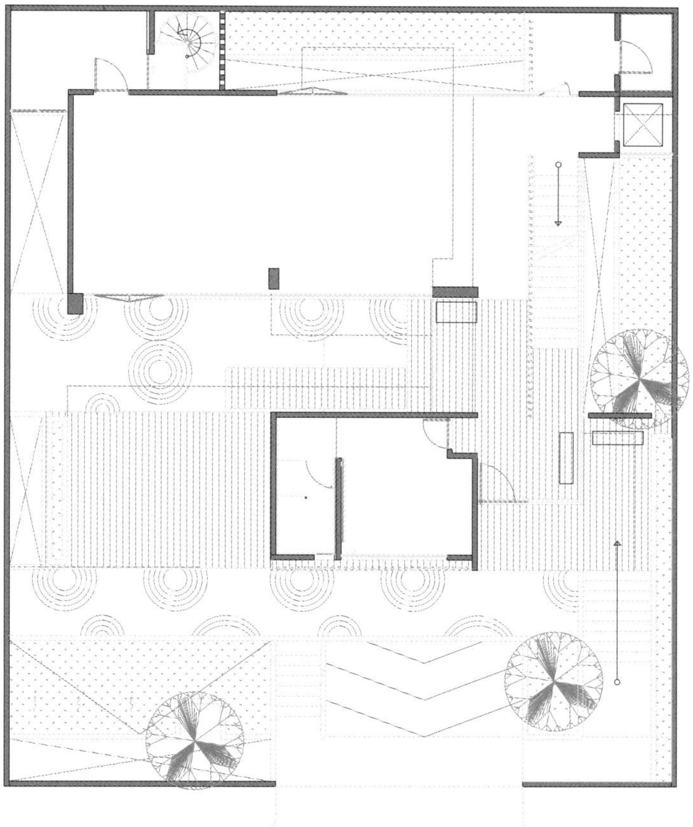

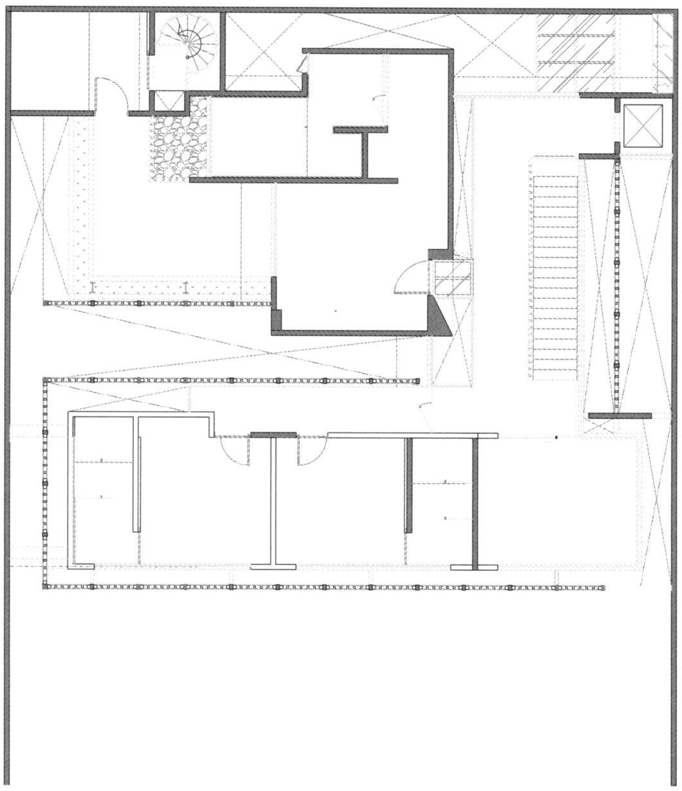

J K

I Exterior view of DS House by night
J First floor plan
K Second floor plan

RADIAL HOUSE

A

OTHER CREATIVES
Field Landscape
YEAR
2020
AREA
1,100 m²
NUMBER OF ROOMS
10
PHOTOGRAPHY
DOF Sky|Ground

Embedded in the hills and the greenery of Khao Yai National Park, this family holiday home is perfectly integrated into the countryside along the river. Conceived for a multi-generation family as a retreat from the city, the residence affords a wonderful panorama view of the lake and the surrounding hills. Divided into two waterside volumes, the incline between the two sections achieves a dynamic connection and is the architecture's most important formal element. The slope-side location enables both connection and partition between the living zones, while the spatial organization provides both independence and privacy. The generous patio enters into a relationship with the natural surroundings and combines with the selected materials, such as raw concrete, wood, and stone, to create autonomous, nature-oriented architecture.

A Aerial view of Radial House
B View of the surrounding nature from the exterior shaped stairs

B

C D

E

F

G

C Terrace with outdoor fireplace
D View from the courtyard of the exterior shaped stairs
E The living room overlooking the lake and courtyard
F Exterior view form the garden
G Top view of Radial House

H

I

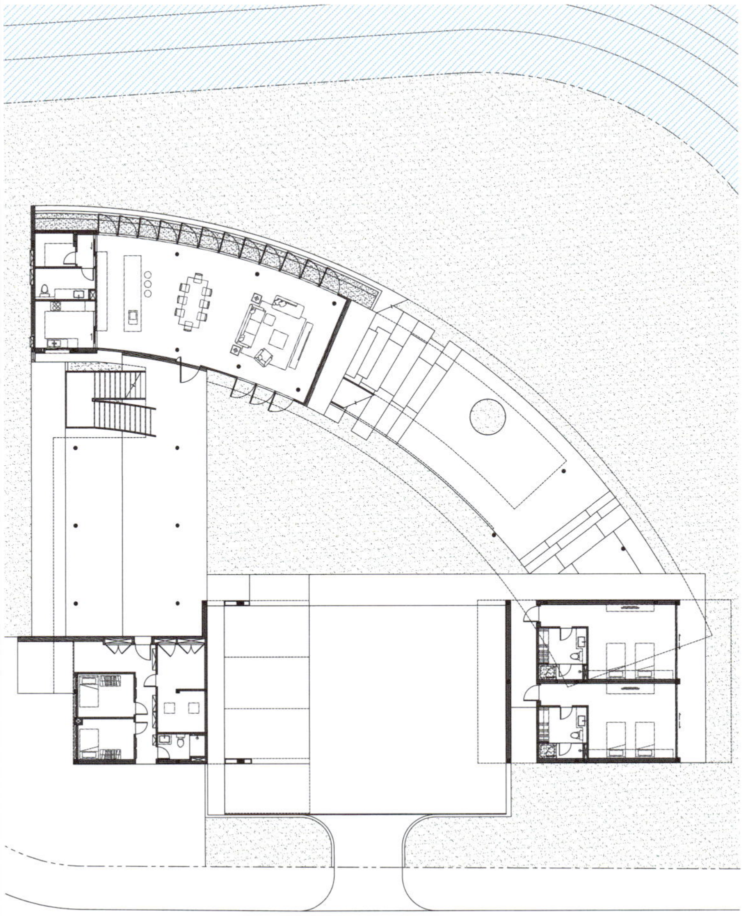

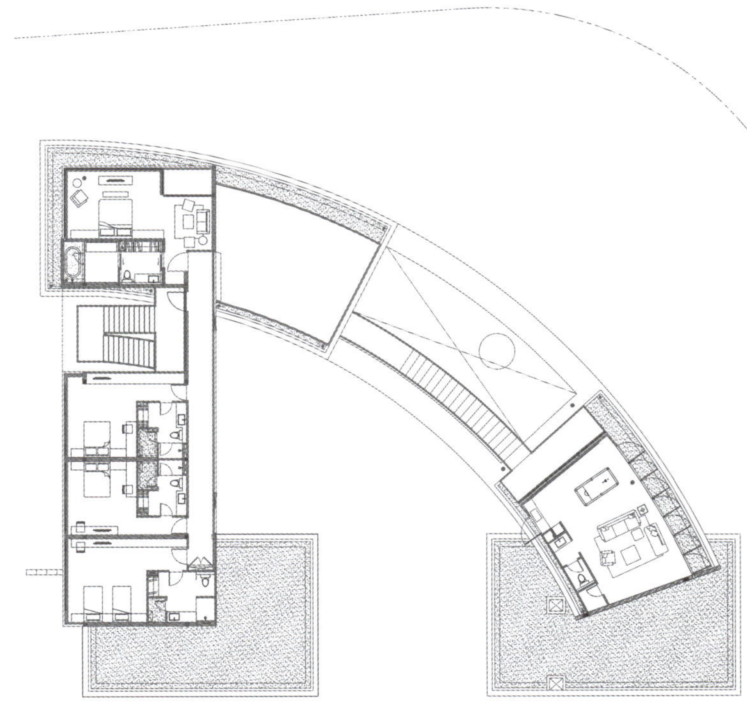

J K

H Front view of Radial House from the water
I View of the dining area open to the garden
J First floor plan
K Second floor plan

HILLSIDE HOUSE

YEAR
2021
AREA
352 m²
NUMBER OF ROOMS
7
PHOTOGRAPHY
Hoang Le

The two-story house is situated on the highest point of the plot, in enchanting surroundings with a breath-taking view of the nearby hills. A sunken path leads to the basement, where the family's vehicles enter the heart of the building. The rooms on the first and second floors are interwoven to create a variety of spaces and a high quality of stay. The structure ensures good lighting and ventilation. A terrace is situated on the mezzanine level, guiding the view of the surrounding hills, while also acting as an eye-catcher from the countryside. The upper level's canopy shields the ground floor from excessive sunlight and provides shady relaxing areas. Between the two floors, a large, open area is created to allow air to circulate inside and interweave the outdoor and indoor spaces. The green, vine-covered building is harmoniously integrated into the tropical environment, its vegetation contributing to a pleasant indoor climate. The interacting open spaces enhance the connection between nature and the building's residents.

A Main view at dusk
B The open and bright interior spaces of Hillside House

B

C

D

C View of the double-height living area
D Aerial view of the house surrounded by nature
E Exterior façade covered with green vines

F Detail of green vines embracing the façade
G Main view of the entrance

F

G

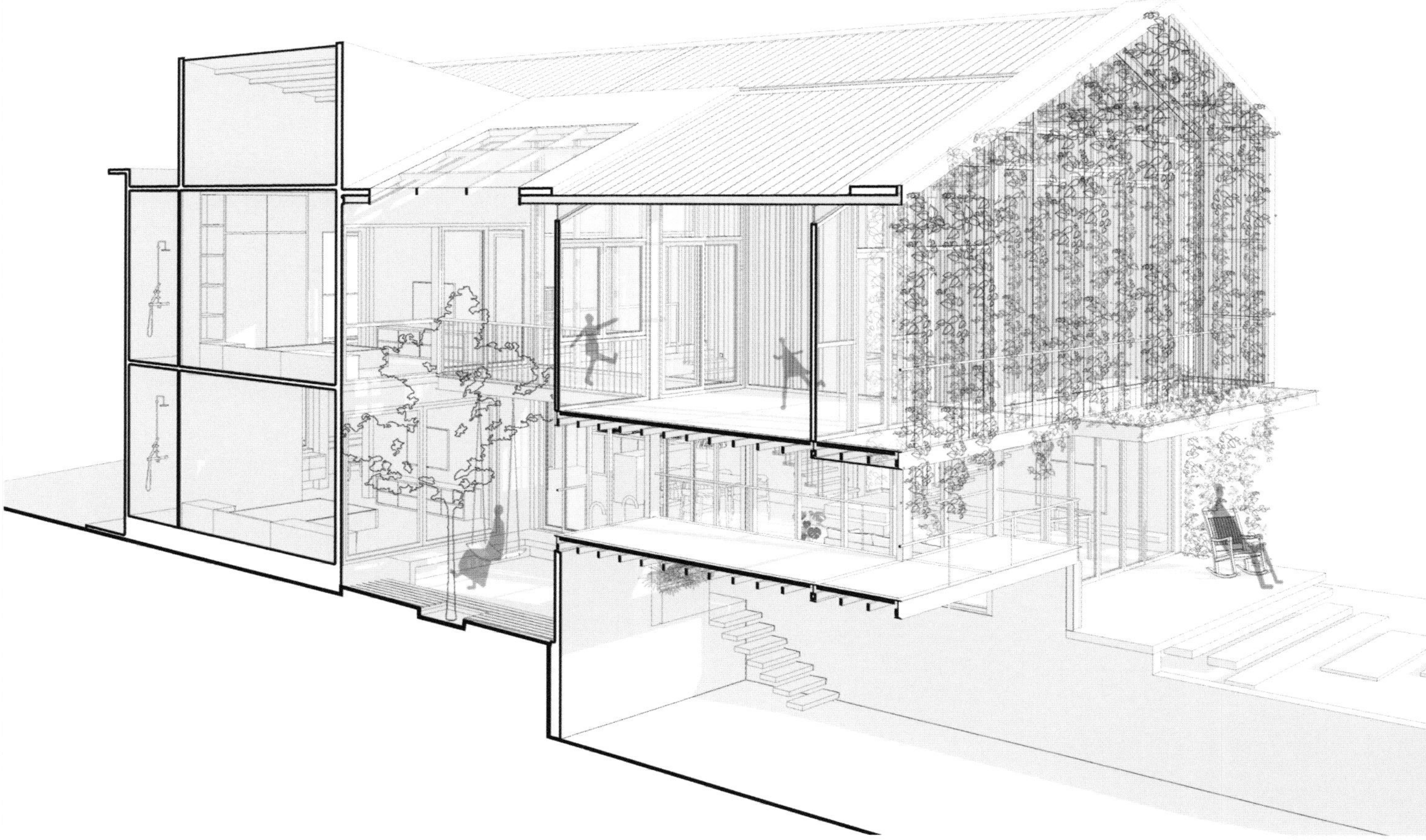

H

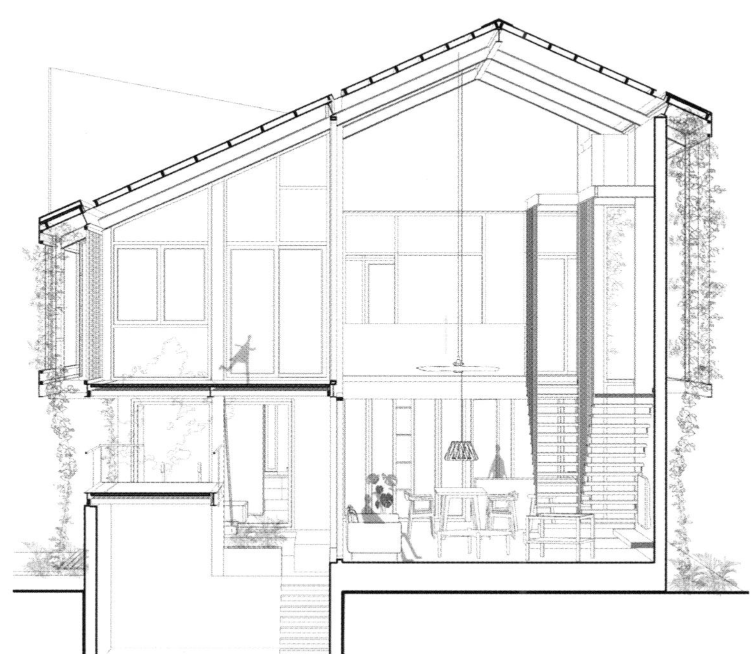

I

H Axonometric cutaway
I Cross section

206

I+I>2 INTERNATIONAL
ARCHITECTURE CONSTRUCTION

MOTHER'S HOUSE

A

207

SƠN TÂY TOWN
VIETNAM

YEAR
2019
AREA
220 m^2
NUMBER OF ROOMS
4
PHOTOGRAPHY
Hiroyuki Oki

Situated in Jackfruit Village on the outskirts of Hanoi, Mother's House expresses a deep connection between humanity and nature. Surrounded by jackfruit, pomelo, and mango trees, the architecture is smoothly integrated into the tree canopies and harmonizes with the greenery. The thatched roof, which is shaped like the back of an aging mother, defies the elements. The raised ground floor enables relaxed walks and improves the natural water drainage. The architecture respects the vegetation and water surfaces, providing a space for the peaceful coexistence of people, animals, and plants. Unfired adobe brick walls and the light thatched roof afford effective protection from the rain and sun, as well as providing noise and heat insulation. The house's curved terrace corridor opens the building's functions up like the embracing arms of a mother. The entire building exudes a friendly, harmonious atmosphere, as light as air.

A Exterior view from above
B Panoramic view of the lake from the covered terrace

B

C Aerial view of Mother's House surrounded by nature

C

D E

F

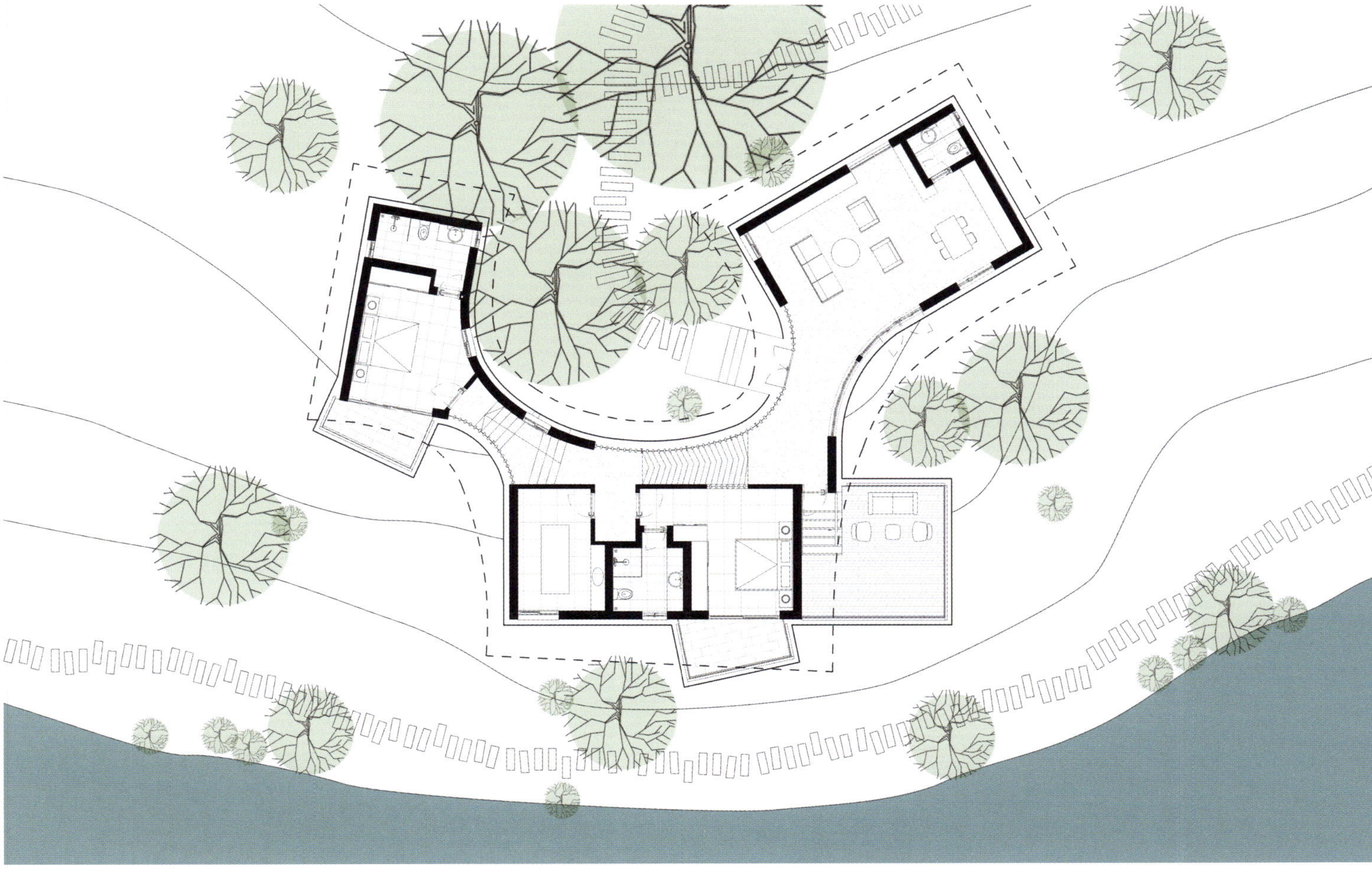

G

H

D View of the large hallway leading to the living area
E Exterior view of the sinuously shaped house
F View of the inner garden surrounded by the house
G Floor plan
H Section detail

K HOUSE

A

OTHER CREATIVES
NORM Architects
YEAR
2018
AREA
350 m^2
NUMBER OF ROOMS
10
PHOTOGRAPHY
Jonas Bjerre-Poulsen, Sri Lanka

AIM Architecture and Norm Architects developed an exclusive villa resort consisting of two buildings in Sri Lanka's Southern Province. The secluded estate directly by the beach is surrounded by lush vegetation and breath-taking views. The architecture's large apertures, soft transitions, and natural materials effortlessly blend in with the landscape. The eastern building on the hilly part of the grounds opens up towards the sea. The western building is more hidden, offering a sheltered atmosphere. Together, the two houses form an L-shape that frames the garden and the central swimming pool. The barn-like structure envelops the outdoor communal zones and opens up the view of the sea. The generous roofs of both buildings protect the interior and exterior spaces from the rain and sunlight, while allowing residents to enjoy the countryside in a shielded and comfortable environment. The materials used create a familiar yet native atmosphere.

A Exterior view of K House from the pool terrace
B View of one bedroom

B

C

C Interior view of the kitchen
D Arial view of K House surrounded by lush greenery
E Outdoor living area open to the surrounding nature
F Detail of the concrete façade with wooden shutters
G View of the dining area

D

E

F G

H

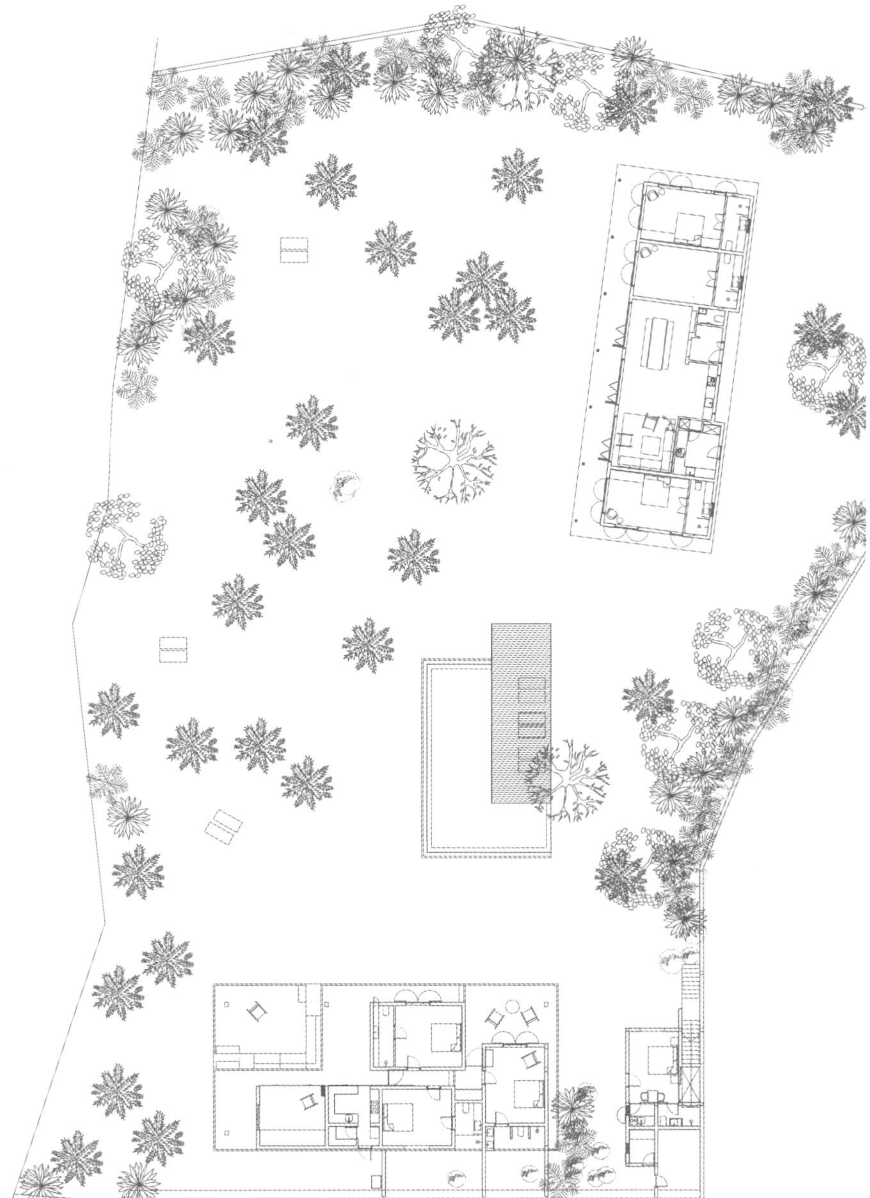

I

H View of K House from the garden
I Site plan

AÇUCENA HOUSE

OTHER CREATIVES
Carlos Maia, Débora Mendes and Igor Macedo as main architects, Laura Georgia Rodrigues Layoun, Octávio Henrique Mendes Pena, Daniele Meloni and Déborah Martins as contributors
YEAR
2021
AREA
500 m²
NUMBER OF ROOMS
5
PHOTOGRAPHY
Jomar Brangança

Açucena House is immersed in a lush Atlantic rainforest and defined by a challenging topography. The project was developed to preserve the location's beautiful natural characteristics. The view of the treetops inspired the concept, elevating the house to allow the flora and fauna below to thrive. No trees were felled and the topography remains unchanged. The architecture adapts to the terrain, achieving a harmonious connection to nature. The white building seems to hover due to its black pillars that merge with the surrounding tree trunks. The fluent floor plan, the result of the trees' position, and the openings and kinks in the ceiling open up the view into the countryside and offer surprising treetop perspectives. Açucena House is like a white flower in the countryside, a unique fusion of art and nature.

A Exterior view of Açucena House
B One bedroom overlooking the surrounding nature

B

C The house surrounded by the nature of the Atlantic rainforest

C

D

E F

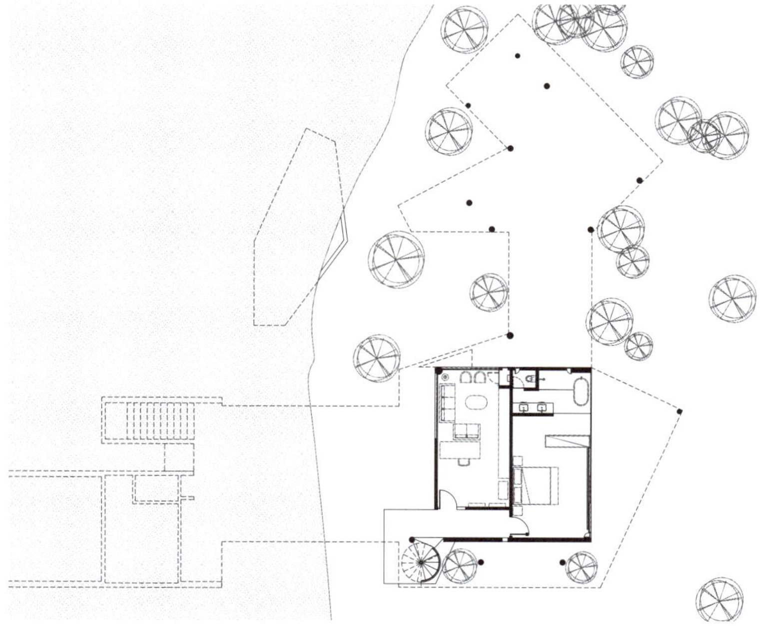

G

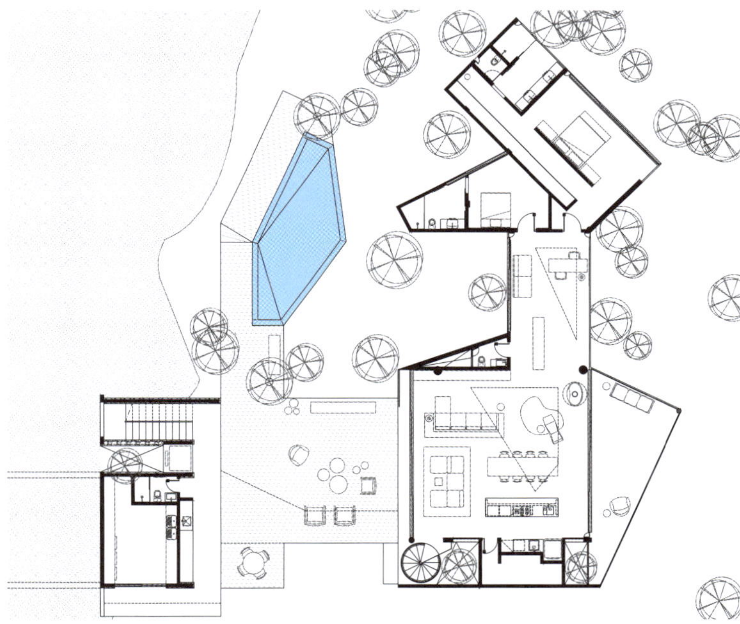

H

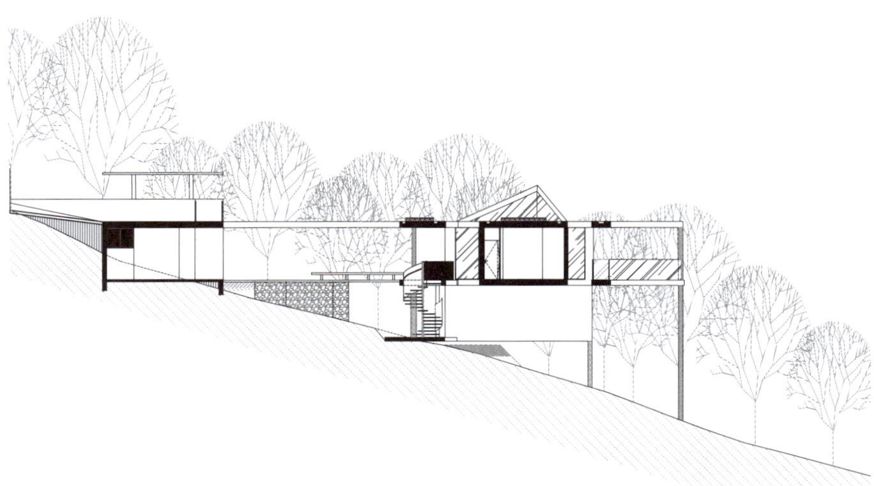

I

D Exterior view from below
E Aerial view of the house surrounded by trees
F View of the floating living room
G First floor plan
H Second floor plan
I Section

VALENTINA AUDRITO
STUDIO AUDRITO

SEASCAPE VILLA

YEAR
2018
AREA
640 m²
NUMBER OF ROOMS
5
FURTHER FACTS
Suspended mezzanine net lounge
PHOTOGRAPHY
Moch Sulthonn for Studio Audrito

The five-bedroom Seascape development is situated directly by the sea on the island of Nusa Lembongan. The design approach is based on the client's desire to create a Mediterranean atmosphere for the villa, which was developed using mainly clean, soft, white volumes, as well as concrete and pebbled floors. A tight footprint had to be worked on due to building restrictions, resulting in a compact two-story structure that houses most of the bedrooms and communal spaces. The guest rooms above the service area are slightly sunken to reduce their impact on the main building. The pool area takes advantage of the elongated plot and connects the building to the beach. The pool's drawn-out appearance is balanced out by the addition of a surrounding deck. Throughout the entire project, the combination of round and square shapes is evident, for instance in the pond design or the wall openings. The materials have an organic feel and are accentuated by the extensive use of bamboo screens to balance the building's very contemporary lines.

A Main view of Seascape Villa from the garden
B Interior view of the kitchen with suspended net lounge

B

C D

E

F

G

C Outdoor bathroom surrounded by bamboo walls
D View of the master bathroom furniture
E Living area of Seascape Villa entirely open to the terrace
F Interior view of one bedroom
G Exterior view of the main entrance from the garden

H

I

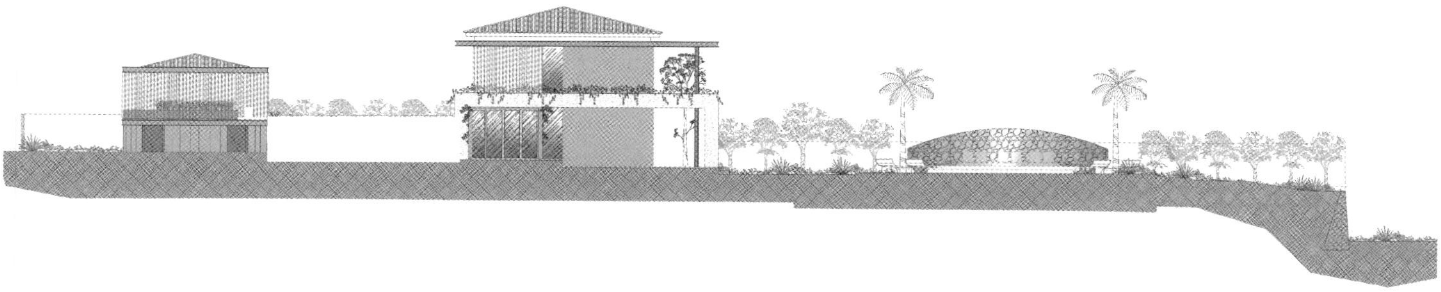

J

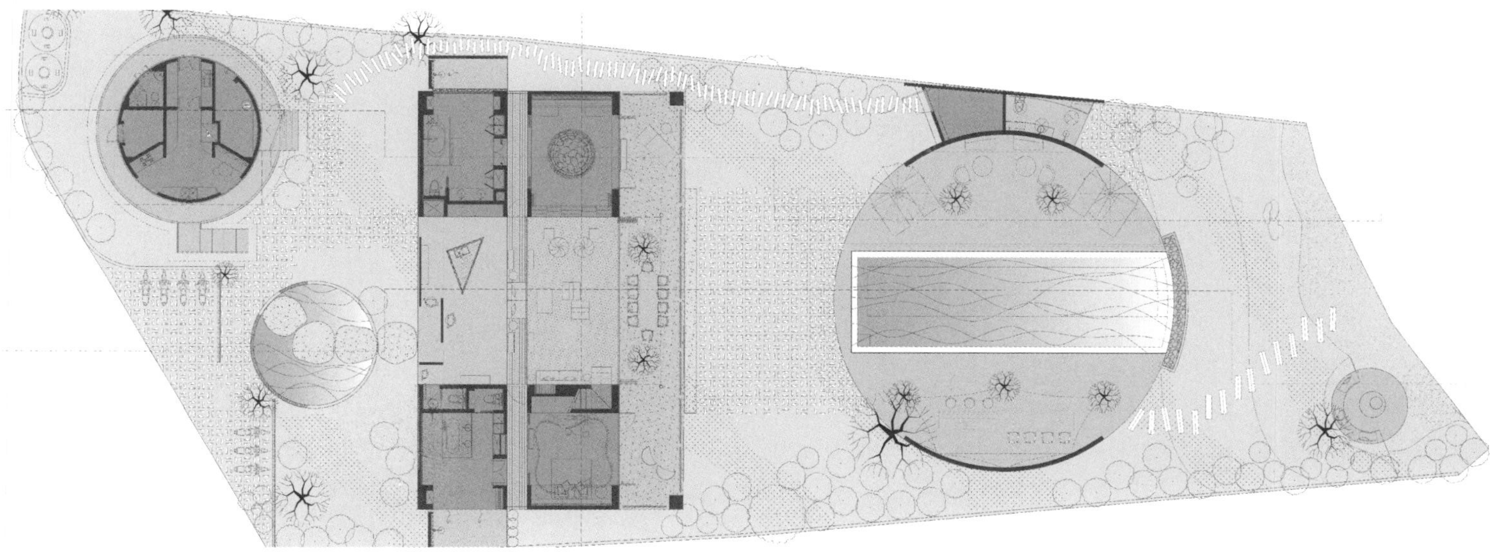

K

H View of the cozy living area
I Main view of the guest bungalow from the garden
J Side elevation
K Site plan

TOQUE-TOQUE HOUSE

231

YEAR
2022
AREA
240 m²
NUMBER OF ROOMS
3
PHOTOGRAPHY
André Scarpa and Pedro Mascaro, São Sebastião

The house in Toque-Toque was conceived as a simple, flexible, and easily constructed building that serves as a summer residence on the São Paulo coast. The plot is situated on a steep slope covered in dense tropical forest. Inspired by this topography, the house was placed perpendicular to the slope, projecting out towards the sea and placing it at the height of the treetops. The location offers a panorama view of the Atlantic Ocean, the island of Toque-Toque and its beautiful beach. The floor-plan arrangement reflects its uses, with peaceful, private areas such as the bedrooms oriented toward the green landscape, while the kitchen and living room face the pool. This allows both areas to enjoy a marvelous view of the sea.

A Aerial view of the House surrounded by nature
B Terrace with infinity pool overlooking the sea

B

C

D

E

F

C Side view of the house
D Living room with large sliding windows overlooking the sea
E Exterior view from the garden
F Basement terrace with tropical forest view

G Aerial view of the house surrounded by nature
H Night view of Toque-Toque House
I First floor plan
J Longitudinal section

G

H

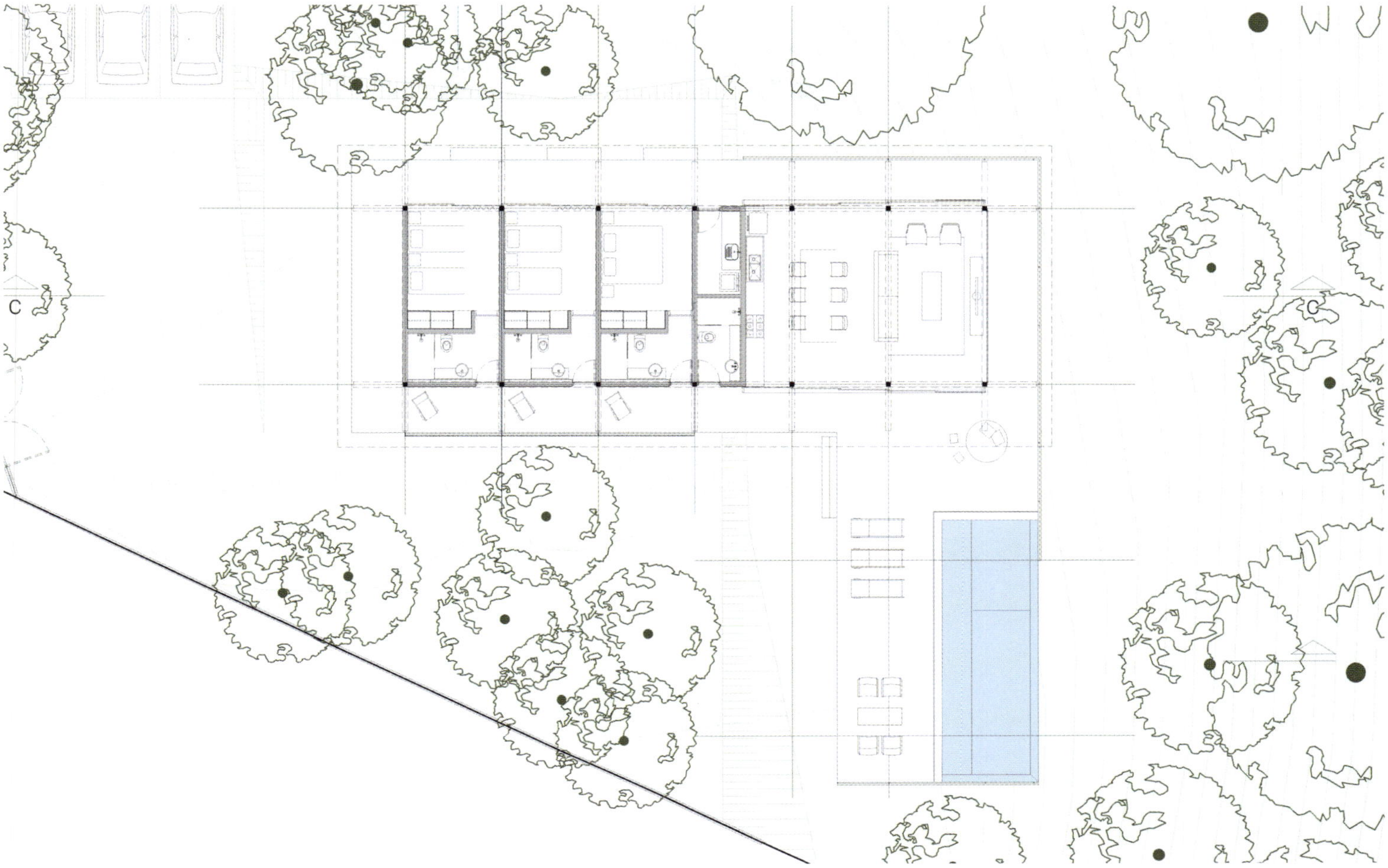

I

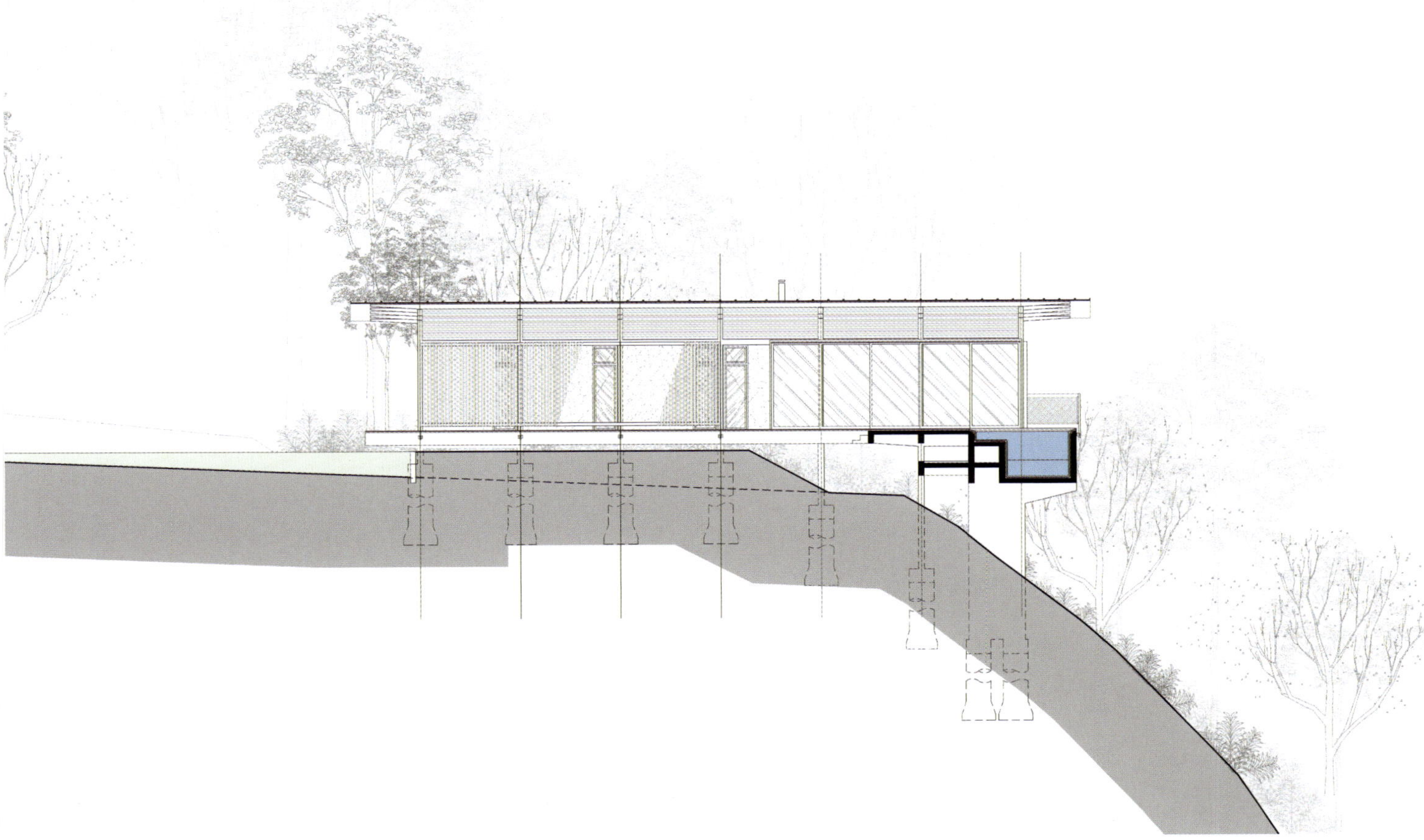

J

A

B

C

D

E

F

G

K

M

N

O

P

R

S

T

V

W

Z

The Deutsche Nationalbibliothek lists this publication in the Deutsche Nationalbibliografie; detailed bibliographic data are available on the Internet at http://dnb.dnb.de

ISBN 978-3-03768-292-0

www.braun-publishing.ch

1st edition 2024

Editor: Sibylle Kramer
Editorial staff and layout: Alessia Calabrò
Translation: Benjamin Liebelt
Graphic concept: Eva Finkbeiner
Reproduction: BildlDruck GmbH, Berlin